GW01551014

CONTENTS

1.1: Muscular skeletal system

1.1.1: Names of muscles and bones. Understanding of the types of movements during physical activities at the regions/joints listed in the table below

What you need to learn: 1.1.1: Names of muscles and bones. Understanding of the types of movements during physical activities at the regions/joints listed.	Yes	Nearly	No
Shoulder - Muscles: Trapezius, anterior and posterior deltoids, pectoralis, latissimus dorsi - Bones: Humerus, clavicle, scapula - Movement: Horizontal flexion, horizontal extension, abduction, adduction, rotation, circumduction.			
Hip - Muscles: Gluteus, hamstring group, psoas major - Bones: Pelvis, femur - Movement: Flexion, extension, abduction, adduction, rotation, circumduction.			
Elbow - Muscles: Bicep brachii, tricep brachii - Bones: Radius, ulna, humerus - Movement: Flexion, extension.			
Leg and knee - Muscles: Quadricep group, hamstring group, gastrocnemius, soleus - Bones: Femur, patella, tibia, fibula - Movement: Flexion, extension.			
Ankle and foot - Muscles: Gastrocnemius, soleus, tibialis anterior - Bones: Tibia, fibula tarsals, metatarsals, phalanges - Movement: Plantar flexion, dorsi flexion, eversion, inversion.			
Wrist and hand - Bones: Radius, ulna, carpals, metacarpals, phalanges			

- **Movement**: Supination, pronation.			
Core and trunk - **Muscles**: Rectus abdominus, latissimus dorsi - **Bones**: Regions of the vertebral column (cervical, thoracic, lumbar, sacral, coccyx) - **Movement**: Flexion, extension, rotation.			

1.1.2: The stretch-shortening cycle, including the different types of contraction/muscular action: isotonic/eccentric, isotonic/concentric and isometric. Application of how movement or stability is produced as a result of these different contractions/muscular actions during physical activity and sporting movements.			
1.1.3: The concept of agonist, prime mover, antagonist, fixator, synergist and how a muscle can take on these different roles when providing stability or movement in a variety of physical or sporting situations.			
1.1.4: The components of an anatomical lever and how the body uses the lever systems (1st, 2nd and 3rd class) in physical activity and sport. This should include the mechanical advantages and disadvantages of each lever.			
1.1.5: Newton's Three Laws of Motion and how they apply to sporting contexts: Law of Inertia, Law of Acceleration & Law of Action and Reaction.			
1.1.6: The principles related to the stability of the body in relation to the centre of mass and its implication in physical activities.			
1.1.7: The calculation of force and resultant force: a mass of 1 kg exerts a force of 9.81 N (down).			
1.1.8: How the muscular and skeletal systems respond, acutely, both structurally and functionally to the stress of warming up and immediate physical or sporting activity.			

POSTERIOR VIEW

Labels (posterior):
- Trapezius
- Medial Deltoid
- Posterior Deltoid
- Triceps brachii
- Latissimus Dorsi
- Gluteus
- Hamstring Group
- Gastrocnemius
- Soleus

Gluteus – extension of the leg at the hip.

Hamstring Gp. – flexion of the leg at the knee.

Soleus – plantar flexion of the ankle when the knee is in flexion.

Trapezius – adducts, rotates, elevates, protracts & depresses the shoulder (scapula).

Medial Deltoid – abduction of the arm at the shoulder.

Posterior Deltoid – extension & lateral rotation of the arm at the shoulder.

Triceps brachii – extension of the arm at the elbow.

Latissimus Dorsi – extension, adduction & medial rotation of the arm at the shoulder.

There are 15 listed in the spec. We have included a couple more to develop understanding further. Focus on names, movements, sporting actions & antagonistic pairs.

Where are they found in the body?

* not on spec. *

LOCATION OF MAJOR MUSCLES

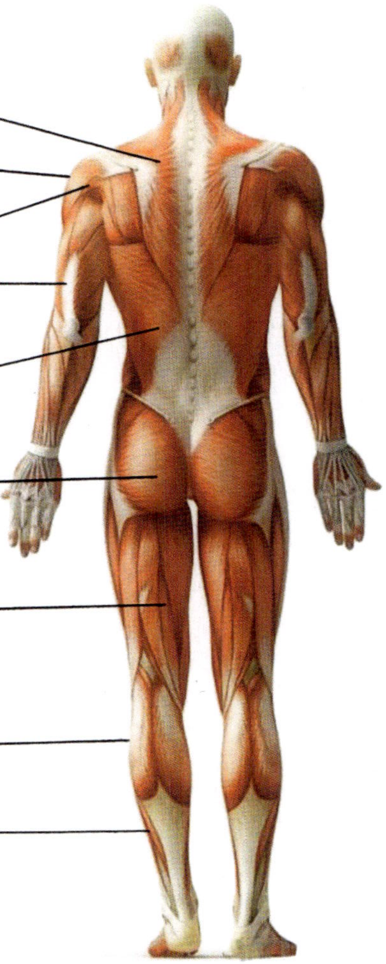

MOVEMENTS

Gastrocnemius - plantar-flexion of the ankle.

ANTERIOR VIEW

Labels (anterior):
- Anterior Deltoid
- Pectoralis
- Bicep brachii
- Rectus Abdominus
- Obliques. *
- Psoas Major. (inside)
- Quadricep Group.
- Tibialis Anterior.
- Gastrocnemius.

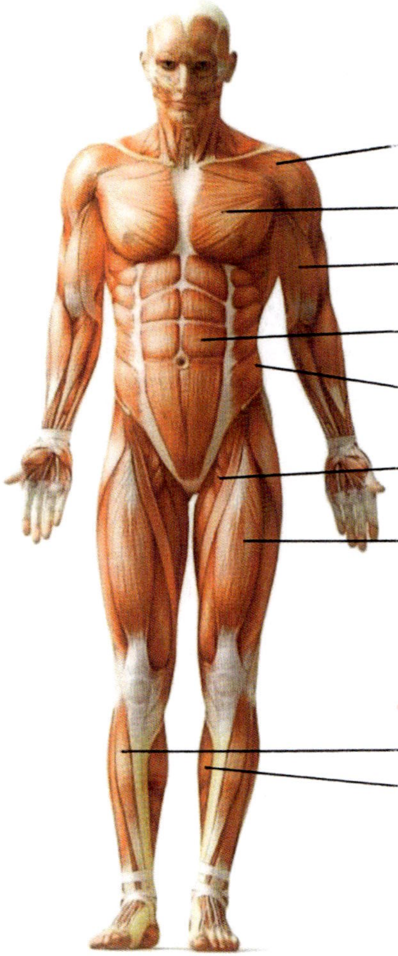

Rectus Abdominus – flexion of trunk at the hip.

Obliques – lateral flexion & rotation of trunk at the hip.

Psoas Major – flexion of the hip.

Quadricep Gp. – extension of the leg at the knee.

Tibialis Anterior dorsi – flexion of the ankle.

Anterior Deltoid – Flexion & rotation of the arm at the shoulder.

Pectoralis – adduction of the arm at the shoulder.

Biceps brachii – flexion of the arm at the elbow.

3

JOINTS, MUSCLES, BONES & MOVEMENTS

ANKLE
JOINT CLASSIFICATION - Gliding
ARTICULATING BONES - Tibia, fibula, tarsals, talus, metatarsals, phalanges
SURROUNDING MUSCLES - Gastrocnemius, soleus, tibialis anterior
MOVEMENTS - Plantar flexion, dorsi-flexion, inversion, eversion

WRIST
JOINT CLASSIFICATION - Condyloid
ARTICULATING BONES - Radius, ulna, carpals, metacarpals, phalanges
SURROUNDING MUSCLES - wrist extensors, wrist flexors.
MOVEMENTS - Supination, pronation

TRUNK
JOINT CLASSIFICATION - Varies depending on region
ARTICULATING BONES - Regions of the vertebral column (cervical, thoracic, lumbar, sacral, coccyx).
SURROUNDING MUSCLES - rectus abdominus, latissimus dorsi
MOVEMENTS - Flexion, extension, rotation.

ELBOW
JOINT CLASSIFICATION - Hinge
ARTICULATING BONES - Humerus, radius, ulna
SURROUNDING MUSCLES - Bicep brachii, tricep brachii
MOVEMENTS - Flexion, extension

KNEE
JOINT CLASSIFICATION - Hinge
ARTICULATING BONES - Femur, tibia, fibula, patella
SURROUNDING MUSCLES - Quadricep Grp, Hamstring Grp, gastrocnemius, soleus
MOVEMENTS - Flexion, extension.

SHOULDER
JOINT CLASSIFICATION - Ball & socket
ARTICULATING BONES - Humerus, clavicle & scapula
SURROUNDING MUSCLES - Trapezius, deltoid (anterior, medial & posterior), pectoralis, latissimus dorsi, rotator cuff (supraspinatus, infraspinatus, teres minor & subscapularis).
MOVEMENTS - Flexion, extension, horizontal flexion, horizontal extension, abduction, adduction, rotation, circumduction

HIP
JOINT CLASSIFICATION - Ball & socket
ARTICULATING BONES - Femur, pelvis
SURROUNDING MUSCLES - Hamstring Grp, gluteus, hip flexors (psoas major & rectus femoris).
MOVEMENTS - Flexion, extension, abduction, adduction, rotation, circumduction

4

JOINT MOVEMENTS

INVERSION
'The movement of the sole towards the median plane.'

Occurs at the ankle (tibia, fibula, tarsals & metatarsals).

Sporting example - turning & carving in ski-ing caused by the contraction of the tibialis anterior where the sole of the foot turns medially.

EVERSION
'The movement of the sole of the foot away from the median plane.'

Occurs at the ankle (tibia, fibula, tarsals & metatarsals).

Sporting example - turning & carving in ski-ing caused by the contraction of the peroneus longus, where the sole of the foot turns laterally.

SUPINATION
'Rotating the forearm into a palm up position.'

Occurs at the wrist (radius, ulna & carpals).

Sporting action - when executing a forehand slice in table tennis caused by contraction of the fore-arm muscles turning the palm upwards.

PRONATION
'Rotating the forearm into a palm down position.'

Occurs at the wrist (radius, ulna & carpals).

Sporting action - when executing a forehand top spin in table tennis caused by contraction of the forearm muscles turning the palm downwards.

DORSI-FLEXION
'Raising the foot upwards (superior manner) towards the tibia.'

Occurs at the ankle (tibia, fibula & talus)

Sporting example - when controlling a pass in football caused by the contraction of the tibialis anterior.

FLEXION
'Decreasing the angle at a joint.'

Occurs at the elbow (radius, ulna & humerus), knee (femur, tibia, patella), hip (pelvis & femur) & trunk (regions of the vertebral column).

Sporting example - Preparing to catch a high ball in rugby caused by the contraction of the biceps brachii.

EXTENSION
'Increasing the angle at a joint.'

Occurs at the elbow (radius, ulna & humerus), knee (femur, tibia, patella), hip (pelvis & femur) & trunk (regions of the vertebral column).

Sporting example - when executing a kick (follow through) caused by the contraction of the quadricep gp.

PLANTAR-FLEXION
'Moving the foot downwards (inferior manner) away from the tibia.'

Occurs at the ankle (tibia, fibula & talus).

Sporting example - when jumping to retrieve a rebound in netball caused by the contraction of the gastrocnemius.

JOINT MOVEMENTS

ADDUCTION

'Movement of a limb towards the mid-line of the body.'

This also occurs at the shoulder (humerus, scapula & clavicle) & hip (pelvis & femur)

Sporting example - when a figure skater brings his/her arms into the body to increase angular velocity when spinning, caused by contraction of the pectoralis.

CIRCUMDUCTION

'Movement of a body region in a circular motion.'

This also occurs at the shoulder (humerus, scapula & clavicle) & hip (pelvis & femur).

Sporting example - when bowling in cricket, caused by the contraction of the deltoids & latissimus dorsi.

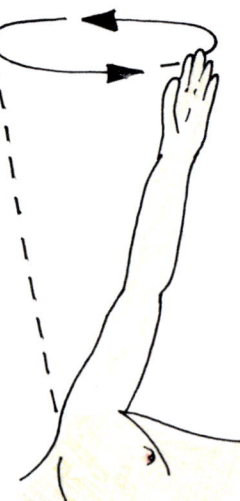

ABDUCTION

'Movement of a limb away from the mid-line of the body.'

Occurs at the shoulder (humerus, scapula & clavicle) & hip (pelvis & femur).

Sporting example - During the preparation phase of the butterfly stroke in swimming, caused by the contraction of the deltoids.

ROTATION

'Movement/pivot/twist around an axis. This occurs at the shoulder (scapula, humerus & clavicle), hip (pelvis & femur) & trunk (regions of the vertebral column).

Sporting example - when hitting a golf ball. During the swing, the trunk rotates (mainly lumbar region) caused by the contraction of rectus abdominus, erector spinae & obliques.

HORIZONTAL FLEXION

'Angle between bones (2) decreases on the horizontal/transverse plane.'

Occurs at the shoulder (humerus, scapula & clavicle).

Sporting example - when executing a forehand shot in tennis by the contraction of the pectoralis & deltoids.

HORIZONTAL EXTENSION

'Angle between two bones increases on the horizontal/transverse plane.'

This also occurs at the shoulder (humerus, clavicle & scapula).

Sporting example - when executing a backhand shot in tennis caused by the contraction of the deltoids, trapezius & latissimus dorsi.

AMORTISATION

- Transition or 'coupling' phase that represents the time between...
  - the eccentric
  - & the concentric phases.

This phase most be kept short as the energy stored during the eccentric phase could dissipate as heat, thereby reducing power output in the next (concentric) phase.

CONCENTRIC

AMORTISATION

ECCENTRIC

Muscle Belly

Achilles Tendon

STRETCH SHORTENING CYCLE (SSC)

- Refers to the 'pre-stretch' that allows an athlete to produce 'more force quickly'.
- It is synonymous with Plyometrics & is often referred to as the 'reversible action of muscles'.

CONCENTRIC

The energy stored during the eccentric phase is used to increase the force produced during the movement.

The force produced is beyond (more than) that of an isolated concentric muscle action.

SSC has **3** phases...

ECCENTRIC or STRETCH PHASE

AMORTISATION or ISOMETRIC TRANSITIONAL PHASE

CONCENTRIC or MUSCLE SHORTENING PHASE

ECCENTRIC

Pre-loading the muscle group(s), while the muscle is lengthening.

Elastic energy is stored, with the tendon being the primary site for storage.

7

MUSCLE CONTRACTIONS

HOW does this work?

When one muscle contracts (shortens) the other relaxes (lengthens) to create movement at a joint. Be specific here, do not just say 'they work together'.

ANTAGONISTIC PAIRS

'Muscles' work in pairs to bring about movement. These are known as ANTAGONISTIC PAIRS. This allows movement in 2 directions. The muscles do not push. Pull on bones, they do not push.

THE AGONIST

This is the muscle that contracts to bring about move-ment. AKA The Prime Mover.

THE ANTAGONIST

This is the muscle opposite the agonist. This muscle relaxes to allow movement to occur.

eg - flexion at elbow.
Trapezius & Rotator Cuff

THE FIXATOR

Muscles that stabilise the origin of the agonist.

THE SYNERGIST

Muscles that stabilise a joint around which movement is occurring.

eg - Flexion at elbow
Brachioradialis

EXAMPLES

BICEPS & TRICEPS - Hinge Joint. Movement occurs at the elbow.

HAMSTRING & QUADRICEP GP - Hinge joint. Movement occurs at the knee.

PSOAS MAJOR & GLUTEUS - Ball & socket. Movement occurs at the hip.

GASTROCNEMIUS & TIBIALIS ANTERIOR - Gliding joint. Movement occurs at the ankle.

Examples

There are **2** main types of muscle contractions.

ISOMETRIC & ISOTONIC

ISOMETRIC

When a muscle is activated or under tension. It does not change length and/or create movement.

eg in an equally weighted rugby scrum, maintaining the crucifix position in gymnastics.

ISOTONIC

Where a muscle shortens / lengthens... it contracts & relaxes under pressure. Creates movement at a joint. Split into 2 types

CONCENTRIC - involves the muscle shortening whilst contracting.

eg the triceps brachii shorten whilst contracting during the execution of a netball shot.

ECCENTRIC - involves the muscle lengthening whilst contracting

eg the quadricep group are under tension & lengthen while in the downward phase of a squat.

8

MECHANICAL ADVANTAGE & DISADVANTAGE

Key Terms

EFFORT ARM - the distance between the effort & fulcrum. The greater the effort arm in comparison to the resistance arm, the greater the mechanical advantage. (1st & 2nd class levers).

However, 3rd class levers have a mechanical disadvantage due to the small effort arm (though allows for quick movements over a large range).

RESISTANCE (LOAD) ARM - the distance between the load (resistance) & fulcrum.

Both 1st & 2nd class levers operate with a mechanical advantage as the fulcrum is closer to the load (a shorter resistance arm) & a longer effort arm, though 2nd class levers have a higher mechanical advantage. A heavier load can therefore be lifted with less effort.

$$\text{Mechanical Advantage (MA)} = \frac{\text{Effort Arm}}{\text{Resistance Arm}}$$

Levers in the body are made up of bones, ligaments, tendons & muscles that enable human movement.

A lever consists of...
FULCRUM - the pivot around which the lever moves (a joint)
LOAD - what you are trying to move (resistance)
EFFORT - the force applied to move the load.
+ **LEVER** arm (bone).

LEVERS

LEVER DIAGRAMS

◢ Fulcrum
▪ LOAD
↑ Effort
▬ Lever Arm

1st class

2nd class

3rd class

Can increase MA through use of equipment - extend resistance arm by using golf club, cricket bat, oar etc.

1ST CLASS

Mimics a seesaw action, where the fulcrum is between the load & effort.

Few in the body, but examples include heading action (at the atlas & axis) & throw in in football.

Flexion at elbow in preparation for throw in.

2ND CLASS

Mimics the use of a wheelbarrow where the load is between the fulcrum & effort.

Like the 1st class lever, these are rare in the body, but can be seen when executing plantar-flexion (running & jumping actions).

3RD CLASS

Represent most joint movements in the body.

The effort is between the load & the fulcrum.

Examples include a squat & upward phase of bicep curl.

1st Law - Inertia

A body continues in it's state of rest or uniform motion unless a force acts on it.

e.g. a ball will not move until a force is applied to it, or it will remain in motion until a player receives it.

Isaac Newton's 3 Laws of Motion are...

1st - Inertia
2nd - Acceleration
3rd - Action/Reaction

2nd Law - Acceleration

The acceleration of an object is directly proportional to the force causing it & is inversely proportional to the mass of the object.

e.g.
m/s^2

force = Mass × Acceleration

$$F = m \times a$$
$$A = \frac{F}{m}$$

The greater the force, the higher the acceleration.

The higher the mass, the smaller the acceleration, therefore a greater force is required.

e.g. a greater force is required to putt a shot in comparison to throwing a cricket ball due to the higher mass of the shot.

Newton's Three Laws of Motion

3rd Law - Action/Reaction

For every action there is an equal & opposite reaction.

e.g. the harder the high jumper applies plantar flexion with the jumping/take off foot, the greater the ground reaction force & so the higher the jump, (considering there are no other limiting factors).

Force

Is the push or pull that impacts an athletes body or an object e.g. force can cause the body or object to...

Speed up - Accelerate
Slow Down - Decelerate
Change Direction

or even...
Change Shape
(hitting a squash ball).

Forces can be generated by the body (internally) e.g. muscular contractions of a 100m runner, or externally e.g. gravity, friction air & water. e.g. gravity & air resistance when high jumping.

10

CENTRE OF MASS - CoM

Is a 'point' that represents the spread of mass of a body.

CoM must be over the base of support if a person is to be balanced (equilibrium)

To increase the stability of an object (reducing the likelihood to topple), the base of support must be increased

for example...

A rugby player can keep their feet wide apart to increase their base of support & bend the knees to lower the CoM. This increases/improves balance & stability, reducing the chance of being tackled.

The 'line of gravity' an imaginary line from the CoM down to the ground must also be in a central position in relation to the base of support.

eg. a batsman playing a leg/offside shot must keep their head still & in line with the ball to reduce leaning too much- bad shot!

This can be manipulated depending on the sporting action. (If you raise your arms, your CoM will also raise/increase in height).

The fosbury flop is an example where the CoM is below the bar on execution (outside of the body) to maximise height, compared to scissors.

CoM

CoM

A force alters the state of motion of a body/object & can be calculated by using... (more on previous page).

force = mass (kg) x acceleration (m/s²)

Newton's — 9.81 N = 1kg

eg. a force needed to move a 10kg mass by 5m/s² can be calculated by:

$$F = ma$$
$$F = 10 \times 5$$
$$F = 50 N$$

TIP - the exam may ask you to calculate acceleration, therefore manipulation of the formula is required.

STABILITY & CALCULATING FORCE

If this object (a) collided with another object (b) that had a force of 75N, the 'resultant (or net) force' would be 25 N & object (b) would win the collision.

RESPONSE TO EXERCISE - MUSCULAR SKELETAL

INCREASED MUSCLE TEMPERATURE

When exercising, playing sport or warming up, the increased supply of blood due to vascular shunting (structural), leads to an increase in muscle temperature (functional). This in turn leads to...

INCREASED MUSCLE PLIABILITY

The 'stretchiness' or elasticity of the muscles increases (structural), which should in turn increase force production & flexibility (functional).

Blood viscosity decreases (structural), which allows for greater/increased blood flow to working muscles & so a greater level of O_2 & dispersion of CO_2 & lactate that cause muscle fatigue. (functional).

Affect either the skeletal system (see left), or the muscular system (the rest). Responses can be either...

Structural - change the make up of body or

Functional - changes the body physiology (response to structural changes).

SKELETAL

There is a simulated uptake of minerals (namely calcium) as a result of weight bearing activity. (functional)
There is a decrease in viscosity of synovial fluid & ... (structural)
An increase in the fluency of joint movement. (functional)

INCREASED BLOOD SUPPLY

Blood vessels that carry oxygen rich blood to working muscles vasodilate (structural). This allows for the blood supply to increase, which in turn allows more O_2 to reach the muscles, thereby allowing the performer to maintain the exercise intensity level (functional)

LACTATE PRODUCTION

Lactate is produced (structural) due to high intensity anaerobic exercise. This occurs when activity rates/levels are above the anaerobic threshold ~80% MHR. Blood pH levels decrease, acidic levels increase, as does H+, which in turn causes fatigue. (functional)

MICROTEARS

Occurs in muscle fibres as a result of high intensity/anaerobic/resistance training (structural) This results in fatigue (functional)
Rest and recovery allows these microtears to 'heal'.

CHRONIC ADAPTATIONS TO EXERCISE - MUSCULAR SKELETAL

INCREASED TOLERANCE TO LACTATE

Comes through specific types of training such as speed/anaerobic endurance or interval. This can increase the lactate threshold, allowing performances to occur at a higher intensity with reduced lactate accumulation & increasing levels of fat oxidisation (use fat as energy)(functional)

MITOCHONDRIAL DENSITY

Increase in size & number (structural) as result of endurance training. Site for aerobic respiration. Whole process becomes more efficient, with an increase in conversion of energy into ATP (functional)

MUSCULAR HYPERTROPHY

An increase in size & diameter of muscle fibres (structural) leads to an increase in muscle size, mass & muscular strength (functional). Mainly due to resistance training.

INCREASED TENDON STRENGTH

With regular exercise, tendons become thicker (structural), stronger & more elastic (functional). Mainly achieved via resistance training & a mixture of eccentric & concentric loading.

INCREASED MYOGLOBIN STORES

Endurance training increases myoglobin stores (structural), increasing the efficiency of O_2 delivery to working muscles. (functional).

INCREASED ENERGY STORES

An increase in energy stores for prolonged/endurance activities. Fat storage increases (structural) as energy increases, & fat used as energy, conserving crucial muscle & liver glycogen for exercise/activity undertaken at higher levels of intensity (functional)

SKELETAL

An increase in bone density & strength (structural) & (functional) due to long term weight bearing activity.

Ligament strength increases (functional). The increased thickness of collagen fibres in the ligaments make them more dense (structural). This in turn....

Increases joint stability & reduces chance of injury (functional)

Articular cartilage increases in thickness (structural)....

which cushions joints during impact & reduces wear & tear of the bone (functional).

1.1: Muscular skeletal system

1. Define the following joint movements.

    a. Abduction. (1 mark)

    b. Pronation. (1 mark)

    c. Inversion. (1 mark)

    d. Extension. (1 mark)

2. Give two muscles that act at the hip. (2 marks)

3. Using examples, describe the difference between horizontal flexion and horizontal extension. (4 marks)

4. Outline how the muscular and skeletal systems work together to enable movement? (3 marks)

5. Outline the difference between an isometric and an isotonic muscle contraction.

6. Explain antagonistic pairs of muscles using a sporting example. (4 marks)

7. Outline each phase of the stretch-shortening cycle. (3 marks)

8. Draw diagrams of each lever system, labelling the key elements involved. (3 marks)

9. Using a sporting example, **explain** why a 2nd class lever has a mechanical advantage. (4 marks)

10. At the start of a 100m sprint, the runner has to push off the starting blocks as quickly as possible to get a good start.

a. Using Newtons First Law of Motion, **explain** how the sprinter pushes off the starting blocks. (2 marks)

b. Using Newtons 2nd Law of Motion, **explain** how the sprinter pushes off the starting blocks. (2 marks)

c. **Calculate** the force needed to allow the sprinter to accelerate if he/she has a mass of 85 kg and at 3.75 m/s/s. (2 marks)

d. Using Newtons Third Law of Motion, **explain** how the sprinter pushes off the starting blocks. (2 marks)

11. **Identify** two ways in which a rugby player can maintain balance in a contact situation. (2 marks)

12. If two footballers collide during a tackle, with player A having a resultant force of 144N and player B 168N, **calculate** the following.

a. Resultant force. (1 mark)

b. If player B was accelerating at 3m/s/s, what was his/her mass (kg). Show working. (2 marks)

13. **Describe** how during a warm-up, two structural muscular-skeletal responses lead to functional benefits in preparation for a performance. (4 marks)

14. **Analyse** the different adaptations achieved on the muscular skeletal system as a result of long-term endurance and strength training. (8 marks)

Total marks for 1.1: Muscular skeletal system. /54

15

1.2: Cardiorespiratory system and cardiovascular systems

What students need to learn	Yes	Nearly	No
1.2.1: Knowledge, understanding and application of the anatomy and physiology of the cardiovascular, circulatory and respiratory systems in physical activity. Understanding of how they function individually and in conjunction with each other.			
1.2.2: The structure and function of the respiratory system to include the larynx, pharynx, trachea, bronchus, bronchiole, alveoli.			
1.2.3: The physiology of the respiratory system as a mechanical process of ventilation (inspiration and expiration). The cause and effect process, including the role of pressure gradients, partial pressure (pp) and diffusion.			
1.2.4: Respiratory values & capacities: tidal volume, inspiratory reserve volume, expiratory reserve volume, residual volume, vital capacity, inspiratory capacity, functional residual capacity, total lung capacity.			
1.2.5: The anatomical components and structure of the cardio vascular system to include, the heart — atria, ventricles, valves, septum, atrioventricular (AV) and sinoatrial (SA) nodes, myocardia — blood, and blood vessels (arteries, veins, and capillaries).			
1.2.6: The physiology of the cardiovascular system with regards to the cardiac cycle, systemic and pulmonary circulation, venous return, vascular shunting, heart rates, (resting, working, maximum, heart rate reserve and recovery), stroke volume, cardiac output, end diastolic and end systolic volumes.			
1.2.7: Understanding of bradycardia, why it may be beneficial and how, anatomically and physiologically, it may occur.			
1.2.8: The cardiorespiratory and cardiovascular systems and how they respond acutely, both structurally and functionally, to the stress of warming up and immediate physical or sporting activity.			
1.2.9: Understanding of what constitutes an unhealthy lifestyle & its effects on the cardiovascular and cardiorespiratory systems.			

STRUCTURE & FUNCTION OF THE RESPIRATORY SYSTEM

① Nasal Cavity
② Epiglottis
③ Pharynx
④ Larynx
⑤ Trachea
⑥ Bronchus
⑦ Bronchioles
⑧ Lungs
⑨ Alveoli
⑩ Diaphragm
⑪ Intercostal Muscles
⑫ Capillaries

NASAL CAVITY - Air is breathed in through the nose the nose. The nasal cavity is divided into 2 by the septum. Air is warmed by mucous membranes, moistened & cilia traps dust & dirt particles (moved to throat to be exhaled).

EPIGLOTTIS - Can be found beneath the tongue. Main/primary role is to prevent food entering the airway. How? Closes over the Trachea.

PHARYNX - Found higher up than Larynx & part of alimentary canal. (Food passes through for digestion) receives food from the mouth & moistens air.

LARYNX - aka the Voicebox. Controls pitch & volume. Contains vocal chords. Air passes through. In the upper Trachea makes sound.

TRACHEA - or windpipe. Made of cartilage. Filters dust same as nasal cavity. c.10cm long, splits left & right to allow air to flow to the Bronchi.

THORACIC CAVITY - a hollow space.

LUNG(S) - Left & right. Form a pair. Extend from clavicle to the diaphragm & contain all pulmonary vessels. One of the major organs. Left slightly smaller due to heart position.

DIAPHRAGM - shaped like a dome. Muscle that separates the thoracic & abdominal cavities. Moves up for expiration, down for inspiration.

INTERCOSTAL MUSCLES - External intercostals attach to each rib. When they contract, rib cage moves up & out. When they relax, rib cage lowers. (to normal position). Internal intercostals - more active during exercise to pull ribs down & more to increase ventilation rate. Works with...

BRONCHUS - One to each lung. Split further into Lobar Bronchi. They split again to form...

BRONCHIOLES - allow for passage of air into...

ALVEOLI - Very important. Air sacs that allow gaseous exchange to occur. Cell walls very thin. Huge capillary network around alveoli, with around 150 million per

CAPILLARIES - site for gaseous exchange

17

THE MECHANICS OF BREATHING

EXPIRATION

The internal intercostals contract & the diaphragm relaxes ①, leading to a decrease in the thoracic space/cavity ②. The size of chest (thoracic cavity) during expiration is highlighted by ③

Pulmonary air pressure becomes higher than the atmospheric pressure & air is therefore expired due to a concentration gradient.

Air goes in.... INSPIRATION
Air goes out.... EXPIRATION

You need to know the process & how the component parts work.

Intercostal muscles (internal & external) Rib cage & diaphragm.

DURING EXERCISE

The process is exactly the same, but the body provides more assistance, with the pectoralis & rectus abdominus & sternocleidomastoid more active.

Breathe In - chest (thoracic cavity) increases in size further allowing more air into the lungs. The pectoralis help pull the rib cage out further & the sternocleidomastoid lifts the sternum

---

Breathe Out -

rectus abdominus assist the ribcage in being pulled down more quickly, though it is the internal intercostal muscles that work to pull the ribcage down more. This helps expel air at a higher, faster rate. An active process with additional fibres & respiratory muscles recruited.

INSPIRATION

There is a higher partial pressure of oxygen (PO_2) in the atmosphere compared to 'in' the lungs.

The external intercostal muscles contract to elevate the ribs ①

The diaphragm then contracts ② (flattens) to increase the thoracic cavity. Pulmonary air pressure is lower than the atmospheric pressure. Movement of air occurs into the lungs due to a concentration gradient.

AT REST

As highlighted above to breathe in. The pressure in the lungs is less than the pressure outside the body, so as the chest (thoracic cavity) expands, the lungs fill with air.

Breathe out - top right. Pressure in the lungs is greater than outside the body, so as the chest (thoracic cavity) reduces in size, air is expelled. Passive process

---

* Read together with next page!

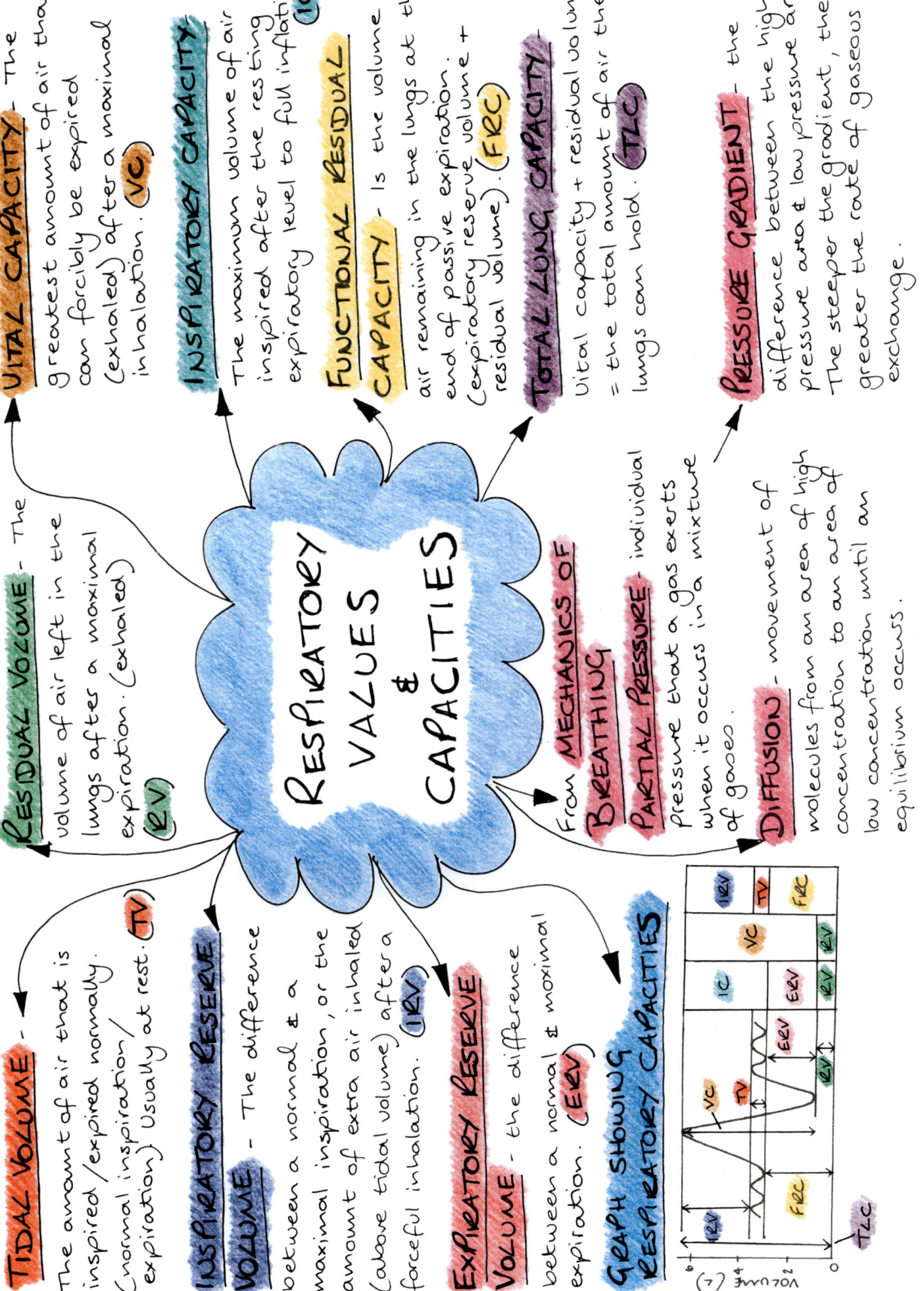

RESPIRATORY VALUES & CAPACITIES

VITAL CAPACITY - The greatest amount of air that can forcibly be expired (exhaled) after a maximal inhalation. (**VC**)

INSPIRATORY CAPACITY - The maximum volume of air inspired after the resting expiratory level to full inflation. (**IC**)

FUNCTIONAL RESIDUAL CAPACITY - Is the volume of air remaining in the lungs at the end of passive expiration. (expiratory reserve volume + residual volume). (**FRC**)

TOTAL LUNG CAPACITY - Vital capacity + residual volume = the total amount of air the lungs can hold. (**TLC**)

PRESSURE GRADIENT - the difference between the high pressure area & low pressure area. The steeper the gradient, the greater the rate of gaseous exchange.

RESIDUAL VOLUME - The volume of air left in the lungs after a maximal expiration. (exhaled) (**RV**)

TIDAL VOLUME - The amount of air that is inspired /expired normally. (normal inspiration/expiration) Usually at rest. (**TV**)

INSPIRATORY RESERVE VOLUME - The difference between a normal & a maximal inspiration, or the amount of extra air inhaled (above tidal volume) after a forceful inhalation. (**IRV**)

EXPIRATORY RESERVE VOLUME - the difference between a normal & maximal expiration. (**ERV**)

MECHANICS OF BREATHING

PARTIAL PRESSURE - individual pressure that a gas exerts when it occurs in a mixture of gases.

DIFFUSION - movement of molecules from an area of high concentration to an area of low concentration until an equilibrium occurs.

GRAPH SHOWING RESPIRATORY CAPACITIES

CARDIOVASCULAR, CIRCULATORY & RESPIRATORY SYSTEMS

PULMONARY CIRCUIT

Carries blood to the lungs from the right ventricle (deoxygenated) at high pressure & oxygenated blood back to the left atrium via the pulmonary vein.

SYSTEMIC CIRCUIT

- Carries blood around the body from the left ventricle (oxygenated) at high pressure & deoxygenated blood back to the right atrium, via the vena cava at low pressure.

- **Venous return** (blood returning back to the heart is at a lower pressure, though is largely dependent on **Cardiac Output** (Q). When Q levels rise, blood is pumped rapidly from the veins. Other factors affecting venous return include...

Skeletal muscle pump - when the muscles contract, the valves are forced to open to increase venous return.

Respiration - during inspiration, venous return increases due to reduced pressure in the thoracic cavity drawing more blood into the right atrium.

Blood volume - an increase in the veins, leads to greater pressure also in the veins. Frank's Starling mechanism means the heart will be able to cope with the increased blood volume. The greater the myocytic stretch, the greater the systolic contraction.

DOUBLE PUMP CIRCULATORY SYSTEM

All **3** systems - (CV, circulatory & respiratory) work together to deliver O2 to the tissues of the body & remove CO2. To do this effectively the systems are divided into **2**. These are...

CARDIOVASCULAR & CIRCULATORY

- Both systems tend to be referred to interchangeably, however to be more technical the CV system includes the heart & blood vessels, whereas the circulatory system refers to the transportation throughout the body - the heart, blood, blood vessels, lymph, lymphatic vessels & glands.

- Both systems are involved in carrying nutrients & hormones to cells, plus removing waste products eg- CO2. Also help protect body from infection & blood loss, maintain constant body temperature (thermoregulation) & maintain fluid balance.

RESPIRATORY

- Is responsible for taking in O2 & dispelling CO2 from the body.
- Is a network of organs & tissue that helps the body to breathe.

Pulmonary Arteries

Low Pressure
Aorta

Highest Pressure

High Pressure

Vena Cava

Lowest Pressure

③ Left Atrium
④ Left Ventricle

① Right Atrium
② Right Ventricle

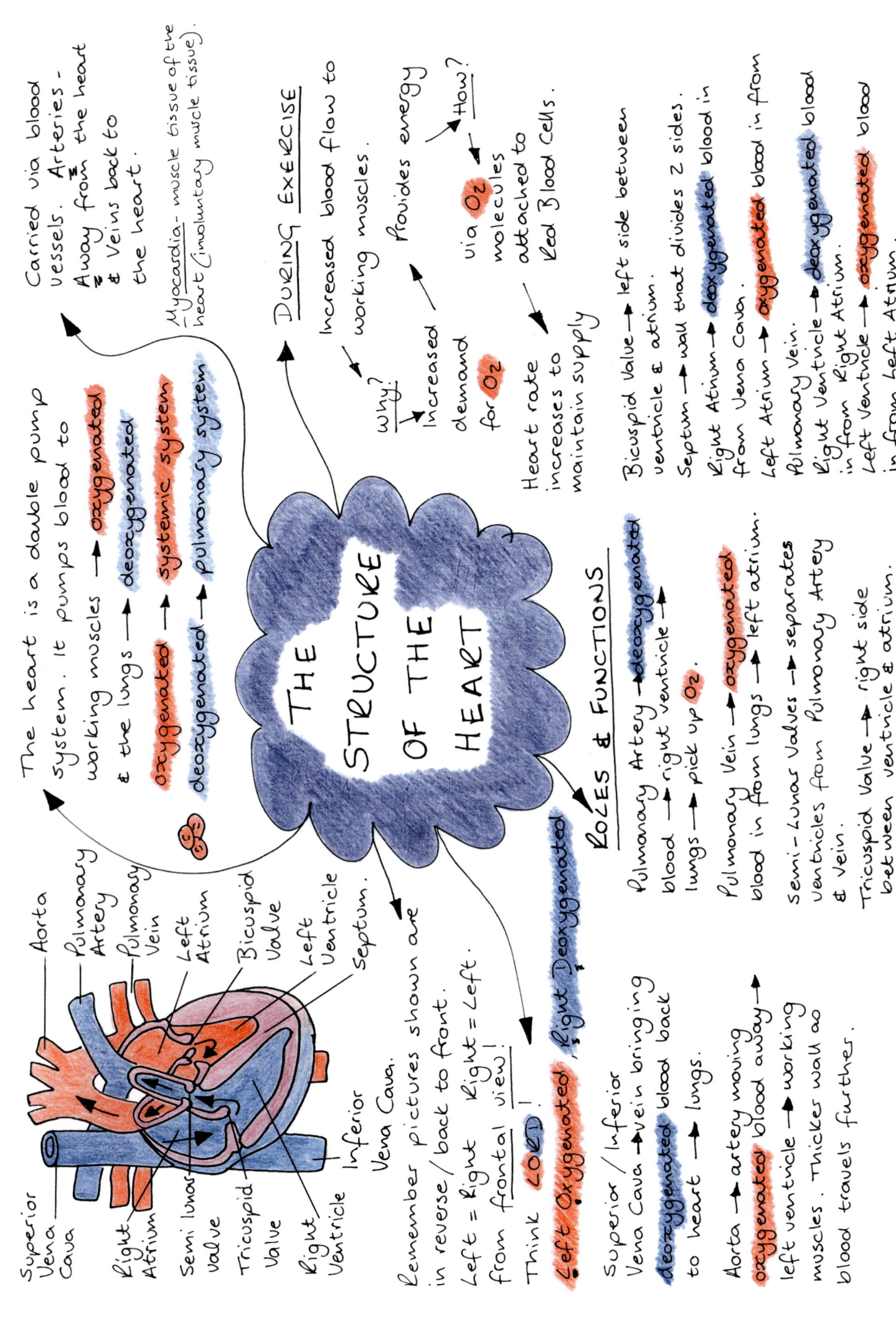

THE STRUCTURE OF THE HEART

Carried via blood vessels. Arteries - Away from the heart & Veins back to the heart.

Myocardia - muscle tissue of the heart (involuntary muscle tissue).

The heart is a double pump system. It pumps blood to working muscles & the lungs → oxygenated / deoxygenated → systemic system / pulmonary system

oxygenated   deoxygenated

DURING EXERCISE

Increased blood flow to working muscles.

Why? → Increased demand for O2

Provides energy → How? via O2 molecules attached to Red Blood Cells.

Heart rate increases to maintain supply

ROLES & FUNCTIONS

Pulmonary Artery → deoxygenated blood → right ventricle → lungs → pick up O2.

Pulmonary Vein → oxygenated blood in from lungs → left atrium.

Semi-lunar Valves → separates ventricles from Pulmonary Artery & vein.

Tricuspid Valve → right side between ventricle & atrium.

Bicuspid Valve → left side between ventricle & atrium.

Septum → wall that divides 2 sides.

Right Atrium → deoxygenated blood in from Vena Cava.

Left Atrium → oxygenated blood in from Pulmonary Vein.

Right Ventricle → deoxygenated blood in from Right Atrium.

Left Ventricle → oxygenated blood in from Left Atrium.

Aorta
Pulmonary Artery
Pulmonary Vein
Left Atrium
Bicuspid Valve
Left Ventricle
Septum

Superior Vena Cava
Right Atrium
Semi lunar valve
Tricuspid Valve
Right Ventricle
Inferior Vena Cava

Remember pictures shown are in reverse / back to front. Left = right, right = left from frontal view! Think LORL!

Left Oxygenated, Right Deoxygenated

Superior / Inferior Vena Cava → vein bringing blood back to heart → lungs. deoxygenated

Aorta → artery moving blood away. oxygenated

left ventricle → working muscles. Thicker wall as blood travels further.

BLOOD VESSELS

Focus on the structure.

- ARTERIES
- ARTERIOLES
- VEINS
- VENUOLES
- CAPILLARIES

Central node

BLOOD & BLOOD VESSELS

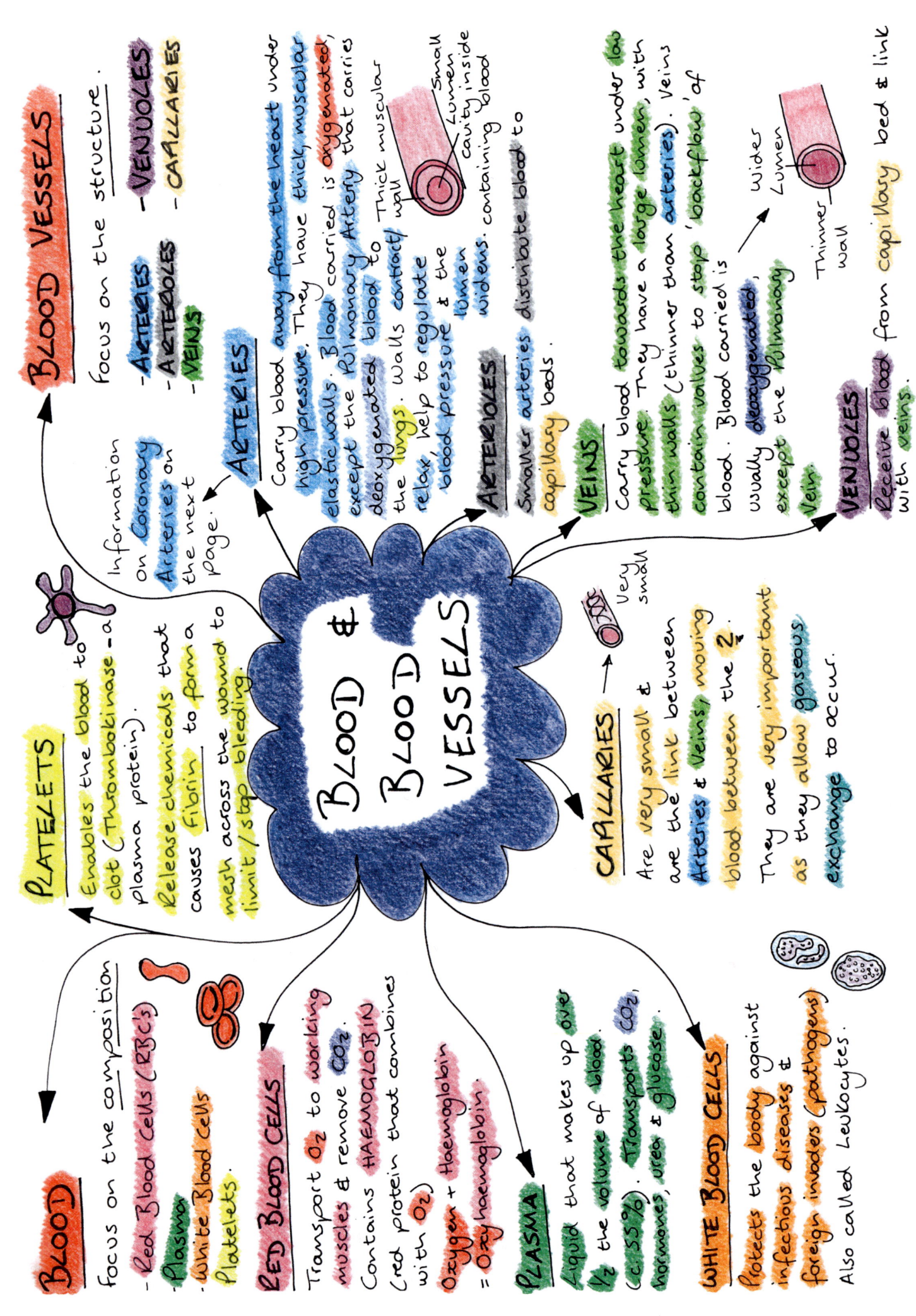

ARTERIES

Carry blood away from the heart under high pressure. They have thick, muscular, elastic walls. Blood carried is oxygenated, except the Pulmonary Artery that carries deoxygenated blood to the lungs. Walls contract & relax, help to regulate blood pressure & the lumen widens.

Thick muscular wall — Small lumen cavity inside containing blood

Information on Coronary Arteries on the next page.

ARTERIOLES

Smaller arteries distribute blood to capillary beds.

VEINS

Carry blood towards the heart under pressure. They have a large lumen, with thin walls (thinner than arteries). Veins contain valves to stop 'backflow' of blood. Blood carried is usually deoxygenated, except the Pulmonary Vein.

Wider Lumen — Thinner wall

VENUOLES

Receive blood from capillary bed & link with veins.

CAPILLARIES

Are very small & are the link between Arteries & Veins, moving blood between the 2.

They are very important as they allow gaseous exchange to occur.

Very small

PLATELETS

Enables the blood to clot (Thrombokinase - a plasma protein).

Release chemicals that causes fibrin to form a mesh across the wound to limit / stop bleeding.

BLOOD

Focus on the composition

- Red Blood Cells (RBC's)
- Plasma
- White Blood cells
- Platelets

RED BLOOD CELLS

Transport O_2 to working muscles & remove CO_2.

Contains HAEMOGLOBIN (red protein that combines with O_2)

Oxygen + Haemoglobin = Oxyhaemoglobin

PLASMA

Liquid that makes up over ½ the volume of blood. (c. 55%). Transports CO_2, hormones, urea & glucose.

WHITE BLOOD CELLS

Protects the body against infectious diseases & foreign invaders (pathogens)

Also called Leukocytes.

22

NERVOUS CONTROL OF THE CARDIAC CYCLE

THE CONDUCTION PROCESS

- **SINOATRIAL NODE (SAN)**
- **ATRIOVENTRICULAR NODE (AVN)**
- **BUNDLE OF HIS**
- **PURKINJE FIBRES**

Nervous impulses & specialist conduction cells initiate the contraction of the heart

An action potential is created by the **SAN** (pacemaker) that travels to the **AVN**, where the impulse is delayed, allowing for passive movement of blood from the atria into the ventricles. (DIASTOLE) This is due to the build up of pressure in the atria that cause the AV valves to open. (Semi -lunar valves are closed)

Exercise speeds up the impulses from the SAN via Sympathetic System increases HR.

The atria contract (ATRIA SYSTOLE) to force blood into the ventricles. However, this only accounts for a fraction of the ventricular filling, because at this point they are almost full.

This decreases the pressure in the atria & therefore the AV valves close. The impulse is conducted to the **bundle of His**, then to the Purkinje fibres. The impulse continues to the apex of the heart & up to the ventricle walls. At this point the pressure has built up in the ventricles.

The ventricles contract (VENTRICULAR SYSTOLE), the semi-lunar valves open & blood is ejected out of the aorta & pulmonary artery.

When ventricular pressure drops below aortic & pulmonary pressures, the semi-lunar valves close, marking the end of the systolic phase & the start of diastole. AV valves are closed & the atria start filling with blood again as the cycle continues.

DIASTOLE - relaxation of heart (0.5 seconds)

SYSTOLE - Contraction of heart (0.3 seconds)

PARASYMPATHETIC

Decreases HR via acetylcholine release.

↓ contraction strength.

Vasoconstriction of arteries → heart & muscles.

Vasodilation of arteries - skin, kidneys & abdomen

SYMPATHETIC

Increases HR via adrenaline/noradrenaline release.

↑ contraction strength.

Vasodilation of arteries → heart & muscles.

Vasoconstriction (some) of arteries - skin, kidneys & abdomen.

CARDIAC DIASTOLE — All chambers relaxed, blood flows into the heart.

ATRIAL SYSTOLE VENTRICULAR DIASTOLE — Atria contract, blood enters into ventricles.

ATRIAL DIASTOLE VENTRICULAR SYSTOLE — Atria relax, ventricles contract, blood is pushed out of the heart.

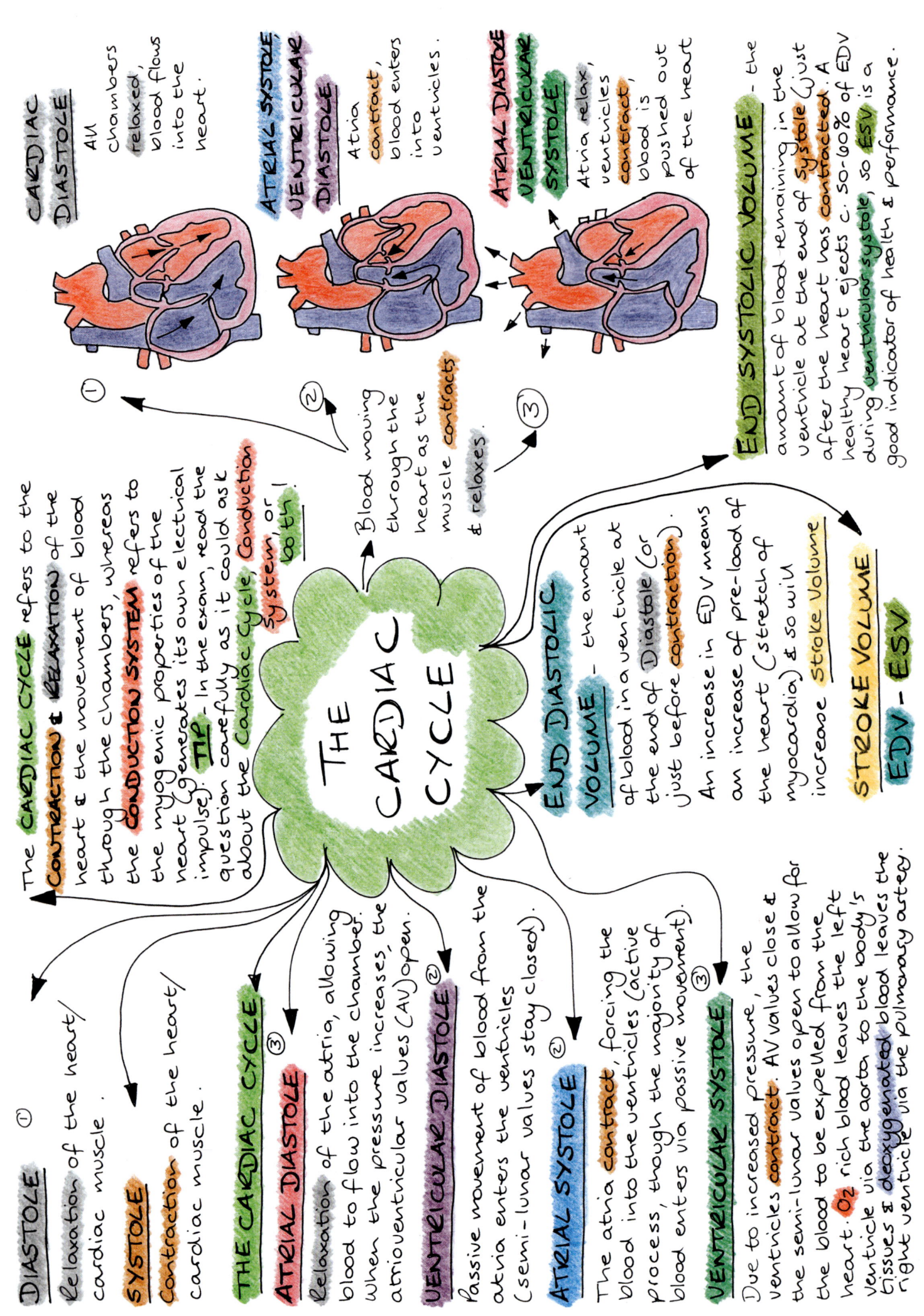

END SYSTOLIC VOLUME — the amount of blood remaining in the ventricle at the end of systole (just after the heart has contracted). A healthy heart ejects c. 50-60% of EDV during ventricular systole, so ESV is a good indicator of health & performance.

The **CARDIAC CYCLE** refers to the **CONTRACTION & RELAXATION** of the heart & the movement of blood through the chambers, whereas the **CONDUCTION SYSTEM** refers to the myogenic properties of the heart (generates its own electrical impulse). **TIP** - In the exam, read the question carefully as it could ask about the Cardiac Cycle, Conduction System, or both!

Blood moving through the heart as the muscle contracts & relaxes.

DIASTOLE ①
Relaxation of the heart/cardiac muscle.

SYSTOLE
Contraction of the heart/cardiac muscle.

THE CARDIAC CYCLE

ATRIAL DIASTOLE ①
Relaxation of the atria, allowing blood to flow into the chamber. When the pressure increases, the atrioventricular valves (AV) open.

VENTRICULAR DIASTOLE ②
Passive movement of blood from the atria enters the ventricles (semi-lunar valves stay closed).

ATRIAL SYSTOLE ②
The atria contract, forcing the blood into the ventricles (active process, though the majority of blood enters via passive movement).

VENTRICULAR SYSTOLE ③
Due to increased pressure, the ventricles contract. AV valves close & the semi-lunar valves open to allow for the blood to be expelled from the heart. O2 rich blood leaves the left ventricle via the aorta to the body's tissues & deoxygenated blood leaves the right ventricle via the pulmonary artery.

END DIASTOLIC VOLUME — the amount of blood in a ventricle at the end of Diastole (or just before contraction). An increase in EDV means an increase of pre-load of the heart (stretch of myocardia) & so will increase Stroke Volume.

STROKE VOLUME
EDV - ESV

THE CARDIAC CYCLE

HEART RATES WHEN
EXERCISING
AEROBICALLY

Graph axes: BPM (vertical) with values 40, 80, 120, 160, 200; Time in mins (horizontal) with values 4, 8, 12, 16, 20, 24, 28. Points labelled 1, 2, 3, 4, 5, 6.

1 - Resting
2 - Anticipatory Rise
3 - steep increase as exercise begins
4 - HR plateaus - steady continuous exercise
5 - Steep decrease when exercise stops
6 - Slowly returns to resting after exercise finished.

(Central bubble) RESPONSE TO EXERCISE

ANTICIPATORY RISE

This is an increase in heart rate prior to the onset of exercise. It is due to the release of neurotransmitters & hormones
- noradrenaline & adrenaline. It prepares the body for exercise.

DEFINITIONS

HEART RATE - the number of times your heart beats in one minute (contracts & relaxes). Ave 60-80 bpm

STROKE VOLUME - the amount/ volume of blood that leaves the heart via the left ventricle per beat. Measured in ml.

CARDIAC OUTPUT - is the volume of blood pumped out of the heart (left ventricle) in one minute.

An increase in heart rate (HR) and/or stroke volume (SV) causes an increase in cardiac output (Q).

This can be worked out as the following equation.

$$Q = HR \times SV \quad l/min$$

eg = 75 x 80ml
= 6,000 ml/min
= 6 l/min.

INCREASED VENOUS RETURN

The amount of blood returning to the heart increases as a result of exercise. The rate of return influences SV & so ultimately Q - more information on page 24 (Systemic Circulation).

INCREASED HR

Beats per minute increases. So too does Stroke Volume. This causes...

INCREASED CARDIAC OUTPUT

There is an overall increase in the volume of blood leaving the heart per minute. Increased Q means higher levels of O₂ rich blood is delivered to working muscles.

INCREASED BP

Increased Cardiac output causes BP to rise, as the larger volumes of blood being delivered put extra pressure on arterial walls.

REDIRECTION OF BLOOD

flow - aka vascular shunting.

During exercise, blood is diverted from 'inactive areas' eg: the digestive system to working muscles - allows athlete to better maintain rate, pace & work intensity.

Responses & Chronic Adaptations – Respiratory System

Increased Vital Capacity

There is an overall increase in the space of the thoracic cavity which allows for an increase in vital capacity, as a greater maximal inhalation can be taken. (functional)

Increased Strength of Respiratory Muscles

There are increased levels of strength & endurance of the diaphragm & intercostal muscles (structural). This allows the body to respire more efficiently & causes an increase in lung capacity. (functional)

Increase in O_2 & CO_2 Diffusion Rate

An increased rate & more importantly efficiency of gaseous exchange at the alveoli. Aided (functional) by...

Increased Capillarisation

There is an increase in the surface area of capillaries surrounding the alveoli. (structural)

Responses – short term

change due to activity.

Chronic Adaptations

impact over a prolonged period of time/more permanent.

Increase in Breathing Rate

During exercise the body will need more air/O_2 to maintain the level of intensity.
Causes an increased rate of inspiration of O_2 & an increased rate of expiration of CO_2.
This can increase from a rate of 12–20 (Average 14) breaths per minute to 40–50 breaths per minute, depending on the activity. (functional)

Increased Tidal Volume

There is an increase in the volume of air moving in & out of the lungs that is available to be used for exercise.
This increase can be as much as 10 times the amount found at rest/normally. (functional)

Increased Gaseous Exchange Rate at the Alveoli

Due to a greater alveolar partial pressure of CO_2 & a lower partial pressure of alveolar O_2 compared to atmospheric pressure the pressure gradient/slope increases allowing for higher rates of gaseous exchange. (functional)

Increase in $\dot{V}O_2$ Max

As a result of improved O_2 delivery & utilisation there is an increase in lactate threshold. (functional)
Allows performer to work at higher intensities for longer (functional) as H+ & lactate accumulation delayed. (structural)

ADAPTATIONS OF THE CV SYSTEM

CAPILLARISATION OF SKELETAL MUSCLE (structural)

Capillarisation causes an increase in number of capillaries & surface area around skeletal muscle & alveoli. This therefore allows for an increase in the rate of gaseous exchange. (functional)

REDUCTION IN RESTING BLOOD PRESSURE (structural)

(Due in part to the improved elasticity of blood vessels. Positive effect on health - less strain on the heart. (functional)

DECREASE IN HR RECOVERY TIME

If more blood rich in O_2 can be transported to working muscles at a faster rate & gaseous exchange is more efficient, then the rate which the heart can recover (back to resting) post exercise is improved. (functional)

INCREASE IN BLOOD VOLUME

An increase in RBC count will increase blood volume. (structural) This can/will have a positive impact on aerobic performance at a higher level of intensity.

DECREASE IN RESTING HR

As the heart can eject more blood per beat, it doesn't have to work as hard / intensely. (functional)

BRADYCARDIA - resting Heart Rate below 60 bpm

CARDIAC HYPERTROPHY

Basically the heart muscle gets bigger & stronger! There is an increase in the thickness of ventricle walls of the heart, particularly the left ventricle. (structural)

This allows for more powerful contractions.

This links to......

INCREASE IN RESTING & EXERCISING STROKE VOLUME (functional)

If the heart contracts more powerfully, it can eject more blood per beat & so stroke volume increases. It allows more blood rich in O_2 to be pumped around the body to working muscles.

This influences the rate of venous return.

Additionally it also affects maximum Q (Cardiac Output). (functional)

27

UNHEALTHY – LIFESTYLES – CARDIOVASCULAR & CARDIORESPIRATORY

Health is defined as... 'the complete state of physical, emotional & social wellbeing, not merely the absence of disease or infirmity.'

An **UNHEALTHY LIFESTYLE** includes habits that lead to a detriment in health. Anything that causes any of the factors to deteriorate would be an unhealthy lifestyle. Factors include...

SMOKING

Increases plaque build up on arterial walls, leading to decreased elasticity in the long term. Reduces the ability to dilate & constrict, leading to an increase in BP (hypertension - chronic effect).

Will eventually lead to a decrease in blood flow & O_2 carrying capacity of RBCs - reducing O_2 delivery to essential tissues & organs.

Respiratory - build up of tar, decreasing surface area of capillaries surrounding alveoli - decrease in diffusion rates.

<u>Long Term</u> - respiratory problems, lung cancer, artherosclerosis, CHD & hypertension.

UNBALANCED DIET

Means an excess or deficiency of the 7 main nutrients. In 'western society', usually due to excess calorific intake, leading to obesity.

Unbalanced diet; high in salt, sugar, saturated fats & LDL cholesterol increases the risk of obesity, hypertension & other hypokinetic diseases.

A balanced diet is recommended with regular aerobic & resistance training. Increases HDL, decreases LDL.

DRUGS

- affect the Central Nervous system - direct influence on how you feel & behave.
Alcohol - socially accepted & legal. Many illegal drugs used 'recreationally' that have a negative impact. eg -

<u>Depressants</u> - slow function of CNS, slow responses & affect concentration eg alcohol, heroin, cannabis.

<u>Hallucinogens</u> - no sense of reality, cause paranoia. eg - ketamine, LSD.

<u>Stimulants</u> - speed up the CNS. Increase HR, BP temperature & anxiety. More alert & confident. eg - caffeine, nicotine, amphetamines.

SEDENTARY LIFESTYLE

A lifestyle involving little or no exercise or activity.

Exercise - physical activity that maintains health & fitness.

Can eventually lead to physiological issues including...
- Muscular atrophy
- Decrease in VO2 max
- Reduction in CoF levels
- Decrease in Basal Metabolic Rate (BMR).

Can also increase the risk of Hypokinetic diseases such as...

- Obesity   - CHD
- Osteoporosis - High BP
- Depression   - Diabetes.

Exercise, namely a combination of aerobic based & weight bearing activity on a regular basis will reduce the incidence of the above.

1.2: Cardiorespiratory system and cardiovascular systems

1. Compare the roles of the systemic and pulmonary circuits.   (4 marks)

2. Identify the following anatomical structures: (3 marks)

   a. Trachea
   b. Bronchus
   c. Diaphragm

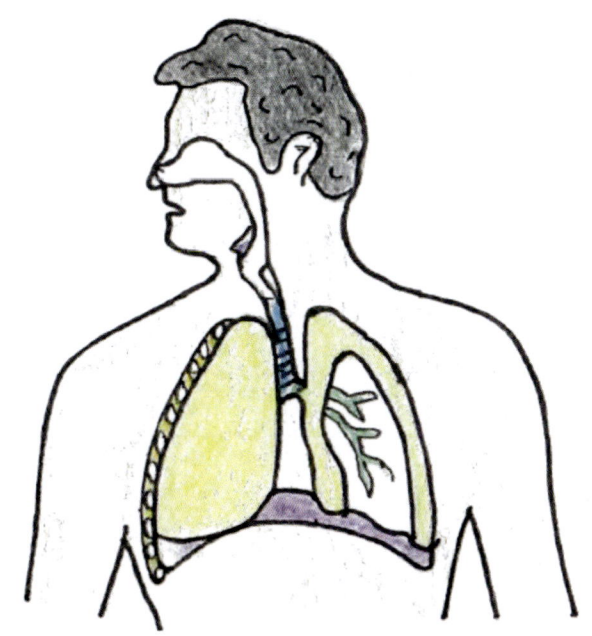

3. Define the following terms:

   a. Expiratory reserve volume   (1 mark)
   b. Residual volume   (1 mark)
   c. Vital capacity   (1 mark)
   d. Inspiratory capacity   (1 mark)

4. **Describe** how gaseous exchange occurs between the alveoli and capillary at rest. (4 marks)

5. **Analyse** the mechanics of breathing at rest. (8 marks)

6. **Define** the following:

   a. Diffusion (1 mark)

   b. Partial pressure (1 mark)

   c. Pressure gradient (1 mark)

7. **Describe** how the cardiovascular and respiratory systems function to allow a sports person to perform to an appropriate level during physical activity. (4 marks)

8. **Label** the following anatomical features of the heart: (5 marks)

   a. Aorta

   b. Pulmonary artery

   c. Right ventricle

   d. Inferior vena cava

   e. Tricuspid valve

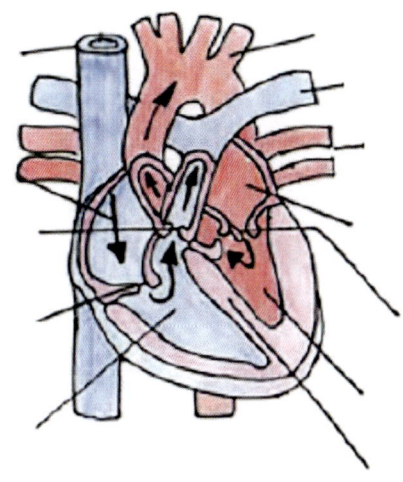

9. **Explain** the changes to stroke volume during a warm-up. **(3 marks)**

10. The figure below illustrates the three major blood vessels.

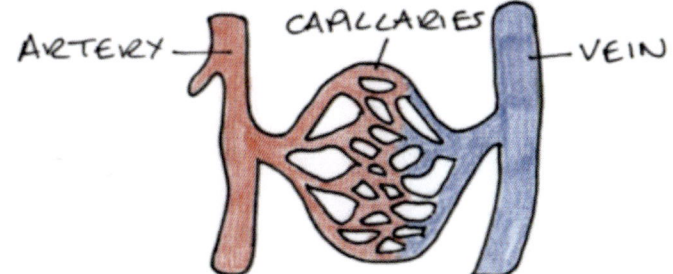

a. **Identify** a structural characteristic for each blood vessel.

(3 marks)

b. **State** how the answer to 'a' influences a functional characteristic.

(3 marks)

Vessel	Structural Characteristic	Functional Characteristic
Artery		
Vein		
Capillary		

11. **Explain** how two respiratory adaptations assist with an endurance performer.

(4 marks)

12. **Define** bradycardia. (1 mark)

13. **Outline** how an unhealthy lifestyle can negatively affect the cardiorespiratory system (4 marks)

14. **Analyse** how the conduction system of the heart controls the cardiac cycle to ensure enough blood is ejected from the heart during the training run. (8 marks)

15. **Evaluate** the adaptations to exercise on the cardiovascular system that would benefit an endurance athlete. (8 marks)

Total marks for 1.2: Cardiorespiratory system: /69

1.3: Neuromuscular system

What you need to learn	Yes	Nearly	No
1.3.1: Knowledge, understanding and application of the anatomy and physiology and the function of the neuro-muscular system during physical activity.			
1.3.2: The characteristics and anatomical make-up of the different fibre types: slow twitch (type I), fast oxidative glycolytic (IIa) and fast glycolytic (type IIx, formerly known as IIb).			
1.3.3: The different structure of each fibre type: how it facilitates their physiology and affects their suitability for particular types of physical activities.			
1.3.4: The fibre recruitment patterns for endurance and power-based events, and how specific training can enable athletes to gain control over the recruitment pattern.			
1.3.5: The anatomy of the neuro-muscular system, including the central nervous system, muscle fibres, myofibrils, sarcomere, motor units, motor neurones and neuro-muscular end plates, the protein filaments of actin and myosin and the roles of globular proteins of troponin and tropomyosin.			
1.3.6: The physiology of a muscular contraction, from a nervous impulse to a muscular response. To include: the neuro-muscular transfer, sliding filament theory, the 'all or none law'. Knowledge of the five stages of a muscle contraction (resting, excitation, contraction, re-charge and relaxing). Understanding of wave summation and gradation of contraction.			
1.3.7: Understanding of how the neuro-muscular system responds acutely, both structurally and functionally to the stress of warming up and immediate physical or sporting activity.			
1.3.8: The chronic adaptations of the cardiorespiratory, cardiovascular, muscular-skeletal and neuro-muscular systems to training.			

ANATOMY OF THE NEURO-MUSCULAR SYSTEM

AXON

Or nerve fibre.
Is a long slender fibre of a motor neuron. It conducts electrical impulses away from the neuron's cell body to the muscle fibre.

NEUROMUSCULAR JUNCTION

Is the site where the axon (axon terminal) of the motor neuron & motor end plate of the muscle fibre/cell meet.

TIP - They do not actually physically meet - there is a gap called the synaptic cleft that separates the axon terminal & the motor end plate.

MOTOR NEURONS

Sometimes called nerve cells. Connected to an axon (nerve fibre) that in turn connects to skeletal muscle.

THE CENTRAL NERVOUS SYSTEM

Consists of the brain & the spinal cord.
Sends signals (or an impulse) called an action potential to a motor unit & travels through a nerve cell (motor neuron).

MOTOR UNITS

Are made up of a single neuron (or nerve cell) that innervates* a group of skeletal muscles. They receive signals from the brain & stimulate all the muscle fibres in that particular motor unit (motor units vary in size).

* innervates = supplies

A MOTOR UNIT

SPINAL CORD

Axons of MOTOR NEURONS

MUSCLE FIBRES

MOTOR NEURON

MOTOR NERVE

35

ANATOMY OF A MUSCLE

SARCOPLASM
Is the cytoplasm of a muscle fibre that contains a network of membranous channels surrounding the myofibrils. It is a water solution containing ATP & phosphagens & contains important organelles, such as mitochondria.

SARCOPLASMIC RETICULUM
The membranous channels that are storage sites for Calcium ions (play an important role in muscle contractions).

MYOFIBRILS
Muscle fibres are made up of many myofibrils bundled together; numerous 'thread-like' structures containing contractile proteins (actin, myosin, troponin & tropomyosin)

SARCOLEMMA
The cell membrane surrounding the muscle fibre.

EPIMYSIUM
The outermost layer of connective tissue that surrounds the entire muscle.

PERIMYSIUM
Connective tissue surrounding the fascicles (individual bundles of muscle fibres).

ENDOMYSIUM
Connective tissue that surrounds each muscle fibre within the fascicles of muscle fibres.

MUSCLE FIBRE
Also known as cells. They are made up of many myofibrils bundled together.

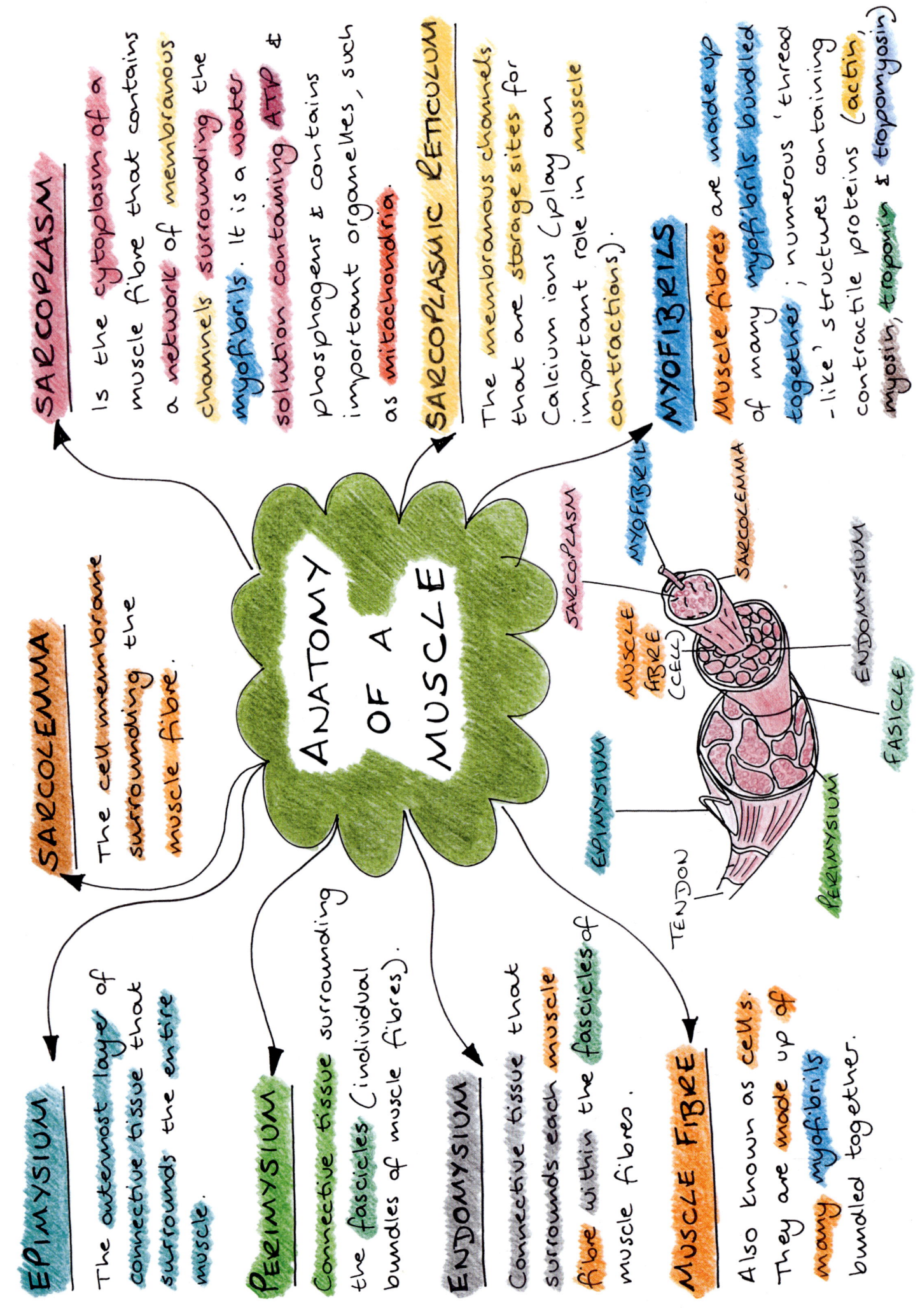

SARCOPLASM
MYOFIBRIL
SARCOLEMMA
MUSCLE FIBRE (CELL)
ENDOMYSIUM
FASCICLE
EPIMYSIUM
PERIMYSIUM
TENDON

ANATOMY OF A MYOFIBRIL

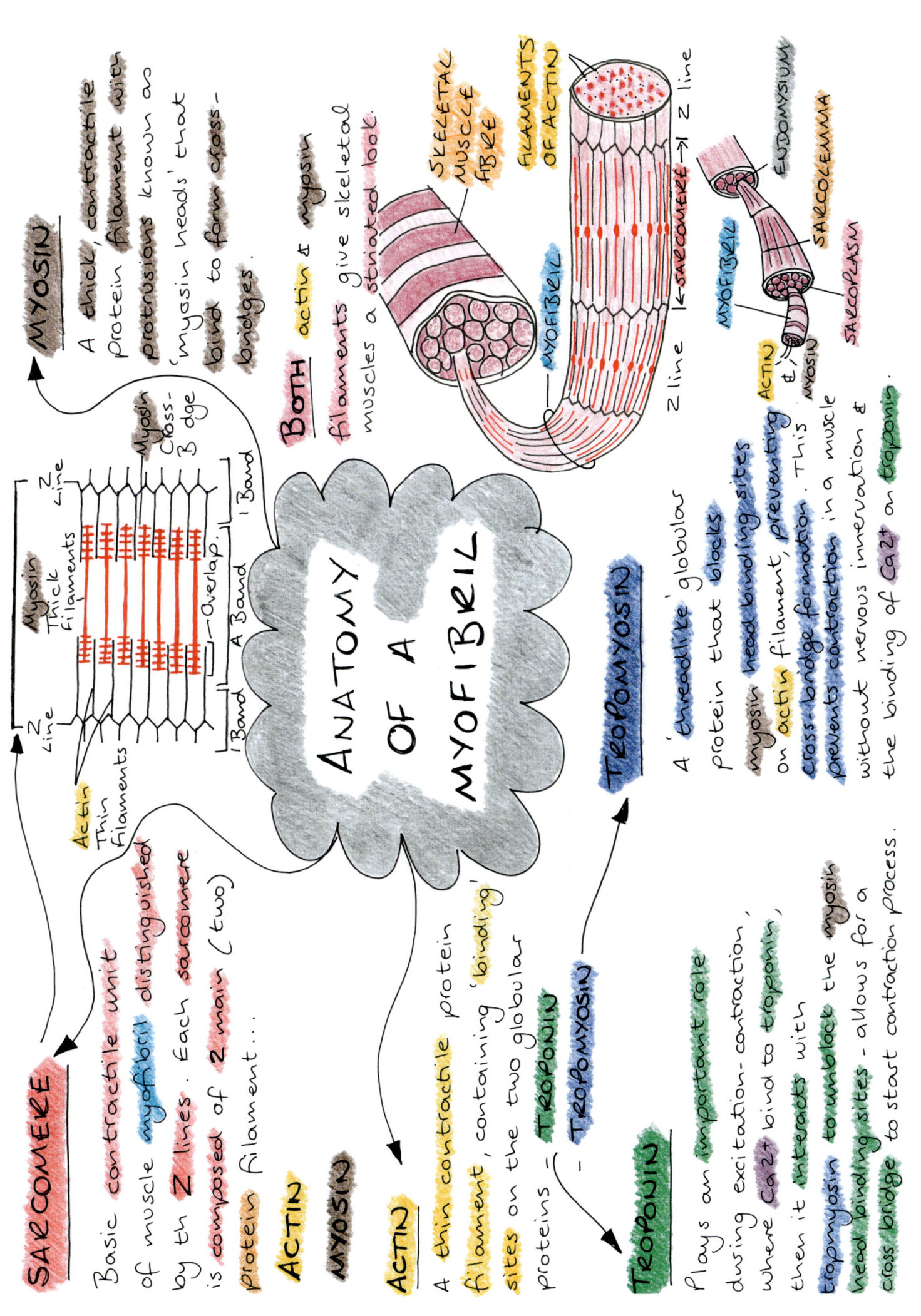

MYOSIN

A thick, contractile protein filament with protrusions known as 'myosin heads' that bind to form cross-bridges.

BOTH

actin & myosin

Both actin & myosin filaments give skeletal muscles a striated look.

Filaments of actin

Myofibril

Skeletal muscle fibre

Endomysium

Sarcolemma

Sarcoplasm

Myofibril

Actin & Myosin

← Sarcomere →

Z line → ← Z line

TROPOMYOSIN

A 'threadlike' globular protein that blocks myosin head binding sites on actin filament, preventing cross-bridge formation. This prevents contraction in a muscle without nervous innervation & the binding of Ca2+ on troponin.

SARCOMERE

Z line
Z line
Myosin Thick Filaments
Actin Thin Filaments
Myosin Cross-Bridge
Overlap
'Band
A Band
'Band

Basic contractile unit of muscle myofibril distinguished by the Z lines. Each sarcomere is composed of 2 main (two) protein filament...

ACTIN

A thin contractile protein filament, containing 'binding' sites on the two globular proteins – TROPONIN – TROPOMYOSIN

MYOSIN

TROPONIN

Plays an important role during excitation-contraction, where Ca2+ bind to troponin, then it interacts with tropomyosin to unblock the myosin head binding sites - allows for a cross bridge to start contraction process.

37

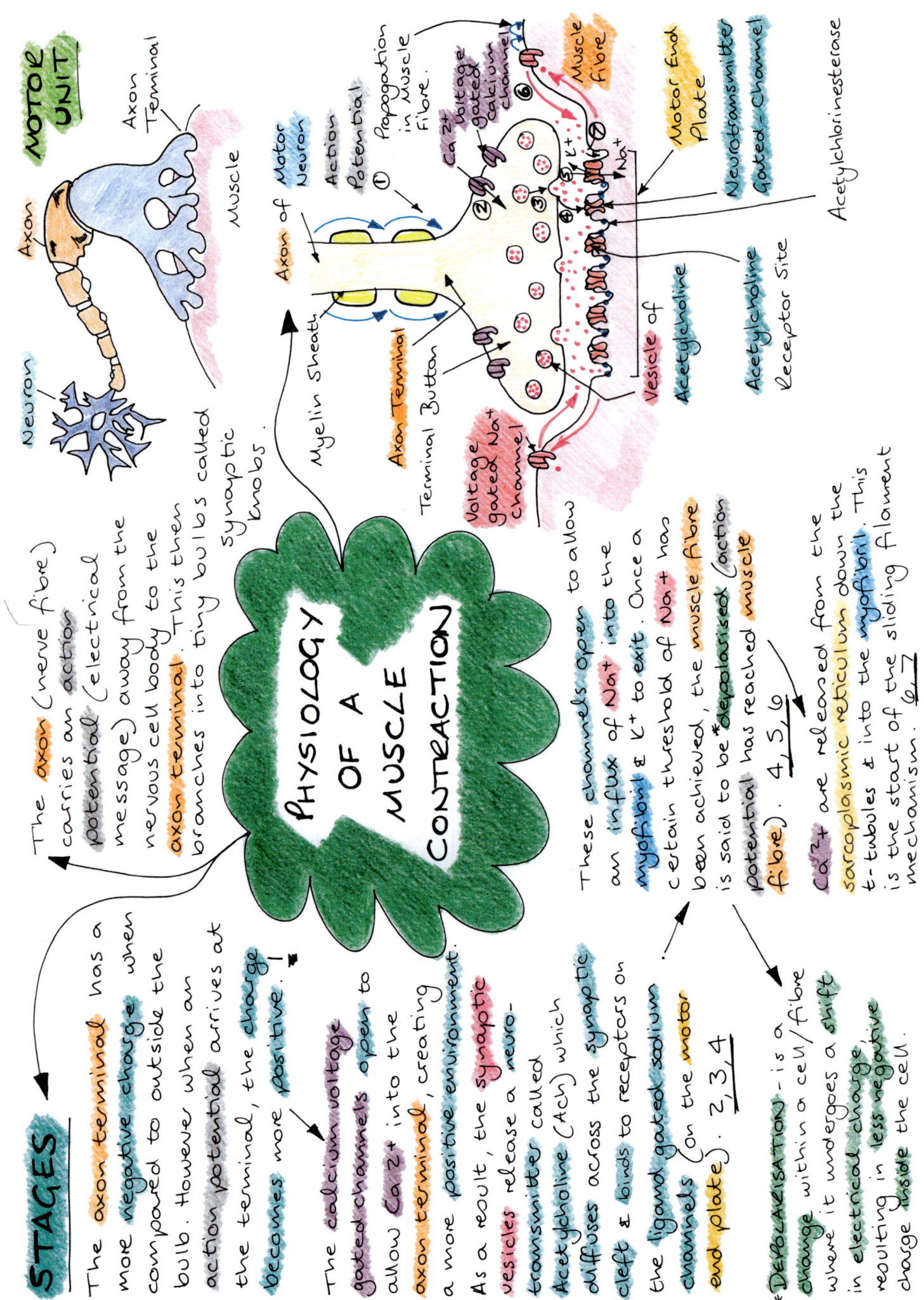

MOTOR UNIT

Neuron

Axon

Axon Terminal

Muscle

Myelin Sheath

Axon of Motor Neuron

Action Potential ①

Propagation in Muscle Fibre.

Axon Terminal Terminal Button

Voltage gated Na+ Channel

Ca2+ Voltage gated calcium channels ⑥

Muscle Fibre

K+

Na+

Motor End Plate

Vesicle of Acetylcholine

Neurotransmitter gated Channel

Acetylcholine Receptor Site

Acetylcholinesterase

PHYSIOLOGY OF A MUSCLE CONTRACTION

STAGES

The axon (nerve fibre) carries an action potential (electrical message) away from the nervous cell body to the axon terminal. This then branches into tiny bulbs called synaptic knobs.

The axon terminal has a more negative charge when compared to outside the bulb. However when an action potential arrives at the terminal, the charge becomes more positive. ①

The calcium voltage gated channels open to allow Ca2+ into the axon terminal, creating a more positive environment. As a result, the synaptic vesicles release a neurotransmitter called Acetylcholine (Ach) which diffuses across the synaptic cleft & binds to receptors on the ligand gated sodium channels (on the motor end plate). 2, 3, 4

*DEPOLARISATION - is a change within a cell/fibre where it undergoes a shift in electrical charge, resulting in less negative charge inside the cell.

These channels open to allow an influx of Na+ into the myofibril & K+ to exit. Once a certain threshold of Na+ has been achieved, the muscle fibre is said to be *depolarised (action potential has reached muscle fibre). 4, 5, 6

Ca2+ are released from the sarcoplasmic reticulum down the t-tubules & into the myofibril. This is the start of the sliding filament mechanism. 6, 7

PHYSIOLOGY OF A MUSCLE CONTRACTION - SLIDING FILAMENT THEORY

The muscle contraction can be explained by these 5 stages...

- Resting Phase
- Excitation Phase
- Contraction Phase
- Recharge Phase
- Relaxation Phase

RESTING PHASE

There is **no** muscle action potential stimulated by the motor neuron, so the muscle is at rest.

Calcium
Thin Filament
Myosin Head
Thick Filament

EXCITATION PHASE

(or excitation-contraction coupling phase).

Ca^{2+} is released into the myofibril & binds to troponin. This causes tropomyosin to move, exposing the binding sites on the actin molecule. ATP on the myosin head hydrolyses & binds to actin, forming a cross-bridge.

ADP
Pi
Cross-Bridges

CONTRACTION PHASE

Myosin cross bridges perform a power stroke (flex - where sarcomere shortens as actin & myosin filament overlap, causing Z lines to move closer to each other).

The energy released by the breakdown of ATP is needed for the power-stroke.

Actin
Calcium binding
P + ADP
Cocking of myosin head
myosin head

Pi + ADP Released
Power stroke

RELAXATION PHASE

When the motor neuron stops firing impulses, Ca^{2+} is removed from the myofibril & stored back into the sarcoplasmic reticulum.

Tropomyosin moves back to cover the active binding sites on actin - no more cross-bridges. The muscle relaxes & returns to it's resting length.

RECHARGE PHASE

ATP is resynthesised & the myosin head detaches from the actin molecule. The process continues as long as there are sufficient levels of Ca^{2+} available to bind to troponin & ATP available for cross-bridge & power-strokes.

ATP attaches to myosin & myosin head detatches.

FIBRE RECRUITMENT PATTERNS

SIZE PRINCIPLE

During voluntary muscle contractions, the orderly pattern of recruitment is controlled by the size of the motor unit.

Small motor units, containing slow twitch muscle fibres have the lowest firing threshold & are recruited first.

Demands for larger forces are met by the recruitment of increasingly larger motor units – Type IIx are recruited last.

Regardless of intensity, slow twitch motor units are recruited first.

Low intensity – these motor units may be the only ones recruited.

High intensity - eg. weight lifting or interval training, slow twitch units are recruited first, then fast twitch IIa, then IIx (if needed).

GRADATION OF CONTRACTION

This refers to the strength or force of contraction exerted by a muscle. Depends on three main factors...

- Recruitment
- Wave summation
- Synchronisation.

ALL OR NONE LAW

A minimum amount of stimulation is required to start a muscle contraction. If an impulse is strong enough, then all the muscle fibres in a motor unit will contract. However, if the impulse is less than the threshold required, no muscle contraction occurs.

The action potential is at full strength or not at all.

RECRUITMENT

Recruitment of fibres refers to the number of motor units stimulated. If only a few motor units within the muscle are stimulated, the strength of contraction will be weak.

The greater the number of motor units that are recruited, the greater the number of muscle fibres that will contract. This increases the force that can be produced. Maximal contraction = All motor units must be stimulated.

WAVE SUMMATION

Frequency of the stimuli. For a motor unit to maintain a contraction, it must receive continuous impulses. Usually a frequency of 80-100 stimuli /sec.

SYNCHRONISATION

If all motor units stimulated at exactly the same time, maximum force can be applied.

Fatigue can be delayed by rotating which units stimulated.

max contract
↑↑↑↑↑ stimuli

TETANIC CONTRACTION

Occurs after several stimuli cause a muscle to contract in rapid succession.

If the stimuli are delivered at high frequency with rest, twitches will overlap.

Tension
Twitch
Wave summation
↑↑↑↑↑↑ stimuli

force
Twitch. Repeated stimulation.

MUSCLE FIBRE TYPES

There are 2 different types
- Slow Twitch - I
- Fast Twitch

Fast Twitch can then be subdivided into......
- Oxidative Glycotic IIa
- Glycotic IIx

FAST TWITCH - also

known as type II. They are needed in sprint, power & strength activities, such as sprinting, jumping, throwing & weightlifting.

They can be subdivided into;
Fast Oxidative Glycotic - IIa
Glycotic - IIx

They contract quickly over a relatively short period of time generating a high level of force & have a low level of resistance to fatigue.

They are pink (IIa) or white (IIx) in colour due to a lower level of O2 supply - work anaerobically.
They have ......

	IIx	IIa
Fibre size	largest	large
Mitochondrial density	lowest	low
Capillarisation	small	moderate
Myoglobin content	low	moderate
PC stores	high	high
Glycogen stores	high	high
Triglyceride stores	low	moderate
Speed of contraction	fastest	fast
Force of contraction	fastest	fast
Resistance to fatigue	lowest	low

Skeletal muscles consist of many (1,000's) of fibres. These fibres differ in their make up physiology, hence different performances in different activities

eg 100m sprinters, 1500m swimmer & a basketball player.

SLOW TWITCH - also

known as type I. They are vital in long distance endurance activities such as swimming, cycling, running & triathlon.

They contract slowly over a prolonged period, generating a low level of force & so have a high level of resistance to fatigue.

They are red in colour due to the high level of O2 supply - work aerobically.

They have ......
- Fibre size - small
- Mitochondrial density - high
- Capillarisation - large
- Myoglobin content - high
- PC stores - low
- Glycogen stores - low
- Triglyceride stores - high
- Speed of contraction - slow
- force of contraction - low
- resistance to fatigue - high

RESPONSES & ADAPTATIONS TO EXERCISE & TRAINING

ADAPTATIONS

ENDURANCE TRAINING

- Results in type IIx muscle fibres being converted into type IIa (though not fully conclusive).

- Increased aerobic capacity of slow twitch muscle fibres due to an increase in mitochondrial density & efficiency of aerobic enzymes.

- Efficiency of the blood supply to the muscles improve slow twitch.

- Increased storage of fat & glycogen.

- Slow twitch muscle activation is more efficient.

POWER TRAINING

- Increased storage of ATP & PC leads to increased strength & efficiency of type IIa & IIx fibres.

- Increased neural firing rates (nerve-muscle connections), timing & co-ordination of recruitment, increase the rate of force production, speed & agility.

- Muscular hypertrophy in fast twitch muscle fibres - greater force produced.

- Hyperplasia - increased number of type IIx fibres.

- Overall increased muscle fibre recruitment (more motor units) to increase force produced.

RESPONSES - short term change due to activity.

ADAPTATIONS - (Chronic) occur over a prolonged period of time / more permanent.

RESPONSES

The benefits of a warm up on the neuromuscular system include...

- Increased number of muscle fibres recruited, leading to increased strength of associated muscles.

- Increased force production, as additional fast twitch muscle fibres are recruited.

- Increased rate of fibre recruitment - speeds up sports related movements & improves co-ordination.

- Type I muscle fibres recruited first as they have the lowest threshold.

- Increased enzyme activity i.e. ATPase & Creatine kinase, leading to more efficient breakdown & subsequent re-synthesis of ATP.

1.3: Neuro-muscular system

1. Skeletal muscle tissue is made up of different fibre types.

   a. **Identify** a structural characteristic for both type I and type IIx muscle
      fibres.   (2 marks)

   b. **Outline** how the structural characteristic in (a) assists with the
      function of type I and type IIx fibres.   (2 marks)

Muscle Fibre	Structural Characteristic	Functional Characteristic
Type I		
Type IIx		

2. **Explain** the suitability of Type IIa fibres to a 400m sprint (running)
                                                                      (6 marks)

3. **Describe** the All or None theory of a muscle contraction. **(2 marks)**

4. **Describe** the size principle of muscle recruitment. **(2 marks)**

5. **Suggest** how the strength of muscular contractions can be altered to ensure a movement is performed correctly? **(4 marks)**

6. **Identify** the following anatomical structures of the neuromuscular system.

   a. Actin **(1 mark)**

   b. Myosin **(1 mark)**

   c. Troponin **(1 mark)**

   d. Tropomyosin **(1 mark)**

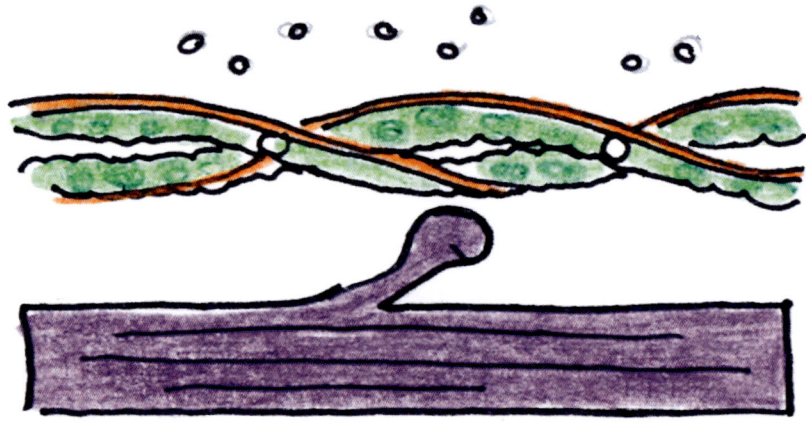

7. **Summarise** the process of a muscle contraction once a muscle fibre has been depolarised. **(6 marks)**

8. Describe the following:

a. Cross-bridge   (1 mark)

b. Power stroke   (1 mark)

9. Explain how three of the structural characteristics of Type IIx muscle fibres enable them to be better suited to power-based activities.

(6 marks)

10. Compare the structural adaptations between endurance and power-based athletes that lead to functional benefits as a result of long-term training.

(8 marks)

Total marks for 1.3: Neuro-muscular system: /44

1.4: Energy systems: fatigue and recovery

What you need to learn.	Yes	Nearly	No
1.4.1: Knowledge and understanding of the concepts of energy, with specific reference to physical activity and sport.			
1.4.2: Understanding of the forms of energy, processes by which it is regenerated, how depletion occurs and the recovery process.			
1.4.3: Forms of energy to include: mechanical, electrical, potential, chemical and kinetic. The role of energy as adenosine triphosphate (ATP) in muscular contraction and the use of phosphocreatine (PC), glycogen and fat as sources for ATP re-synthesis.			
1.4.4: The characteristics and physiology of the three energy pathways (ATP-PC, glycolytic and aerobic).			
1.4.5: The characteristics of the three pathways with regards to ease and speed of ATP production, the force of contraction that each will support, the intensity and duration of exercise supported by each as the dominant energy provider and the regeneration of ATP for each pathway.			
1.4.6: The principle of the energy continuum when based around athletic running events.			
1.4.7: Use of the continuum as a medium to support understanding of the joint and collaborative role of the three energy pathways in physical activity.			
1.4.8: Positioning of athletic running events on the energy continuum.			

1.4.9: The concept of fatigue and factors that contribute to fatigue: energy depletion, dehydration and the build-up of waste products (which should include an exploration of the role of lactic acid in performance).			
1.4.10: Stages of recovery and their application to specific physical and sporting contexts.			
1.4.11: The fast component of recovery and re-phosphorylisation; the speed and rate of phosphogen replenishment.			
1.4.12: The slow component of recovery; the oxidation of lactate (removal of lactate and H+), replenishment of energy stores and the two hour window of opportunity: rehydration, physical cooling and thermoregulation; the 48- hour window of opportunity: resaturation of myoglobin, re-synthesis of protein, glycogen and carbohydrate (CHO), exercise induced muscle damage (EIMD) and delayed onset muscular soreness (DOMS).			
1.4.13: EPOC (excess post-oxygen consumption), and the stages of recovery.			
1.4.14: Understanding of how the energy systems respond acutely, to the stress of warming up/priming exercise.			

Concepts & Forms of Energy

Energy Sources include...

PHOSPHOCREATINE – PC
Phosphocreatine stores are vital/essential in replenishing ATP stores.

The fuel used in the Alactic or PC system. Only enough to last 7-10 seconds. eg. 100m sprint.

GLYCOGEN
Stored version of carbohydrate (CHO) & utilised as glucose in both aerobic & anaerobic energy pathways.

Provides an efficient source of energy as the body requires less O_2 to burn CHO compared to fat or protein. Vital during high intensity activity.

FAT
Provides more than twice the potential energy than protein & CHO.

Helps fuel low-mid intensity exercise, utilising the aerobic energy system.

Can help with endurance activities (run, swim, cycle) if the body is conditioned properly as it spares the use of muscle & liver glycogen stores for high intensity activity.

PROTEIN
Last resort of energy to be used (as major source) in the aerobic system.

Body breaks down amino acids found in skeletal muscle leading to the breakdown of lean muscle tissue.

Provides energy in the later stages of prolonged exercise. eg. ultra - marathon.

Forms include...

MECHANICAL
Is the energy of an object due to its motion or position. It is the sum of Potential & kinetic energy.

eg. applying energy by using force on the pedals to move a bike.

ELECTRICAL
Is the movement of charged particles. eg. nerve impulses/action potentials, ions.

POTENTIAL
Is stored energy that when released is converted into kinetic energy. eg. Potential energy stored in ATP.

CHEMICAL
Energy produced from chemical reactions. eg. when ATP is hydrolysed.

KINETIC
Energy that an object possesses due to its motion. This depends on both its mass & velocity.

eg. kinetic energy is released from the Potential energy of a tennis racquet when a ball is hit during the ball's flight.

48

THE ROLE OF ATP IN EXERCISE

It is the **ENERGY CURRENCY** of the body, a high energy compound.

It is the chemical form of **ENERGY**

ATP is.... **A**denosine **T**ri **P**hosphate

There is sufficient **ATP** stored in the muscles for roughly 2-3 seconds of work. Then what?

It must be resynthesised (constantly) so that a continuous supply of energy can be had.

How? The resynthesis occurs either at rest or during steady/moderate aerobic activity over a prolonged period.

Energy from the breakdown of **PC-ATP** forms

Creatine Kinase

P/C → creatine + Pi

A-P-P

A-P + energy + Pi

When ATP is hydrolysed (broken down), Adenosine Diphosphate is created, plus an inorganic phosphate as **ENERGY** being released from the 'broken' bond

A-P-P-P → A-P-P + P + energy

ATPase

For movement to take place (during exercise), the body must move **STORED** energy into **MECHANICAL** energy.

ATP molecules are made up of atoms held together with a set of bonds. These bonds are highly charged.

A-P-P-P

Breaking the 'outer' bond causes the energy to be released to fuel many/all body functions & processes, including muscle contractions (skeletal muscle) - vital for exercise to occur!

The various types of **ENERGY** systems that are used when bonds are broken will be discussed over the following pages.

THE AEROBIC SYSTEM

The process of AEROBIC respiration

AEROBIC GLYCOLYSIS

PYRUVATE COENZYME A

ACETYL COENZYME A

CITRIC ACID

KREB'S CYCLE

CO_2

Hydrogen Carriers
- $NADH_2$
- $FADH_2$

$H+ e-$
$H+2$ Hydrogen & carbon atoms transported to inner membrane of mitochondria.

ELECTRON TRANSPORT CHAIN (ETC)

$H+$ oxidised

2 ATP

34 ATP + CO_2 + H_2O

YIELD 36 ATP

YIELD - 36 ATP

SITE - Mitochondria

FUEL - Glycogen

DURATION - > 90 seconds

RECOVERY - 1-3 days depending on duration & intensity of activity.

AEROBIC
Meaning 'in the presence of oxygen.'

SUITABLE SPORTS
All long distance / endurance activities.

eg - marathon running, 1500m swim, triathlon, long distance cycling.

MITOCHONDRIA
Are the powerhouses within muscle cells.

Breaks down glucose molecules under AEROBIC conditions.

Slow twitch muscle fibres have more mitochondria than fast twitch muscle fibres. They are able to provide energy for a longer period of time.

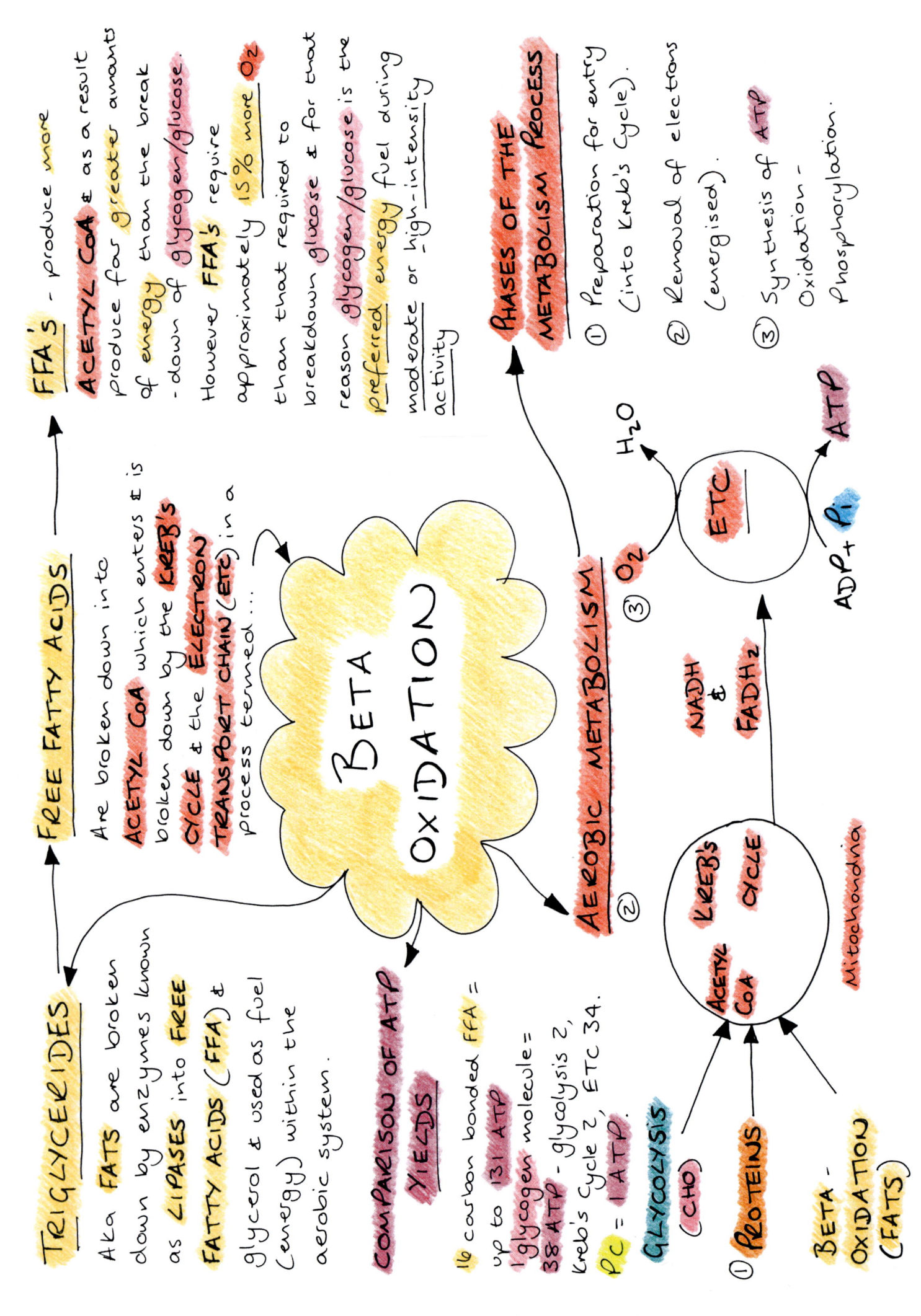

FFA's – produce more **ACETYL CoA** & as a result produce far greater amounts of energy than the break -down of glycogen/glucose. However **FFA's** require approximately 15% more O_2 than that required to breakdown glucose & for that reason glycogen/glucose is the preferred energy fuel during moderate or high-intensity activity

PHASES OF THE METABOLISM PROCESS

① Preparation for entry (into Kreb's Cycle).

② Removal of electrons (energised).

③ Synthesis of ATP – Oxidation – Phosphorylation.

FREE FATTY ACIDS

Are broken down into **ACETYL CoA** which enters & is broken down by the **KREB'S CYCLE** & the **ELECTRON TRANSPORT CHAIN (ETC)** in a process termed...

BETA OXIDATION

AEROBIC METABOLISM ② O_2 ③

H_2O

ETC

ADP + P_i → **ATP**

NADH & FADH₂

KREB'S CYCLE

ACETYL CoA

Mitochondria

TRIGLYCERIDES

Aka **FATS** are broken down by enzymes known as **LIPASES** into **FREE FATTY ACIDS (FFA)** & glycerol & used as fuel (energy) within the aerobic system.

COMPARISON OF ATP YIELDS

16 carbon bonded FFA = up to 131 ATP

1 glycogen molecule = 38 ATP - glycolysis 2, Kreb's Cycle 2, ETC 34.

PC = 1 ATP.

GLYCOLYSIS (CHO)

① **PROTEINS**

BETA - OXIDATION (FATS)

Requires you to understand the positioning of athletic running events on the **ENERGY CONTINUUM**.

REMEMBER...

It is the **DURATION** or **TIMING** of each event that determines the relative % of each energy system used, **NOT** the distance!

DISTANCE	200	400	800	1500	5000	10000	30m
TIME	22	49	1m53	3m55	14m	30m	
% AEROBIC	29	43	66	84	95	97	
% AN-AEROBIC	71	56	34	16	5	3	

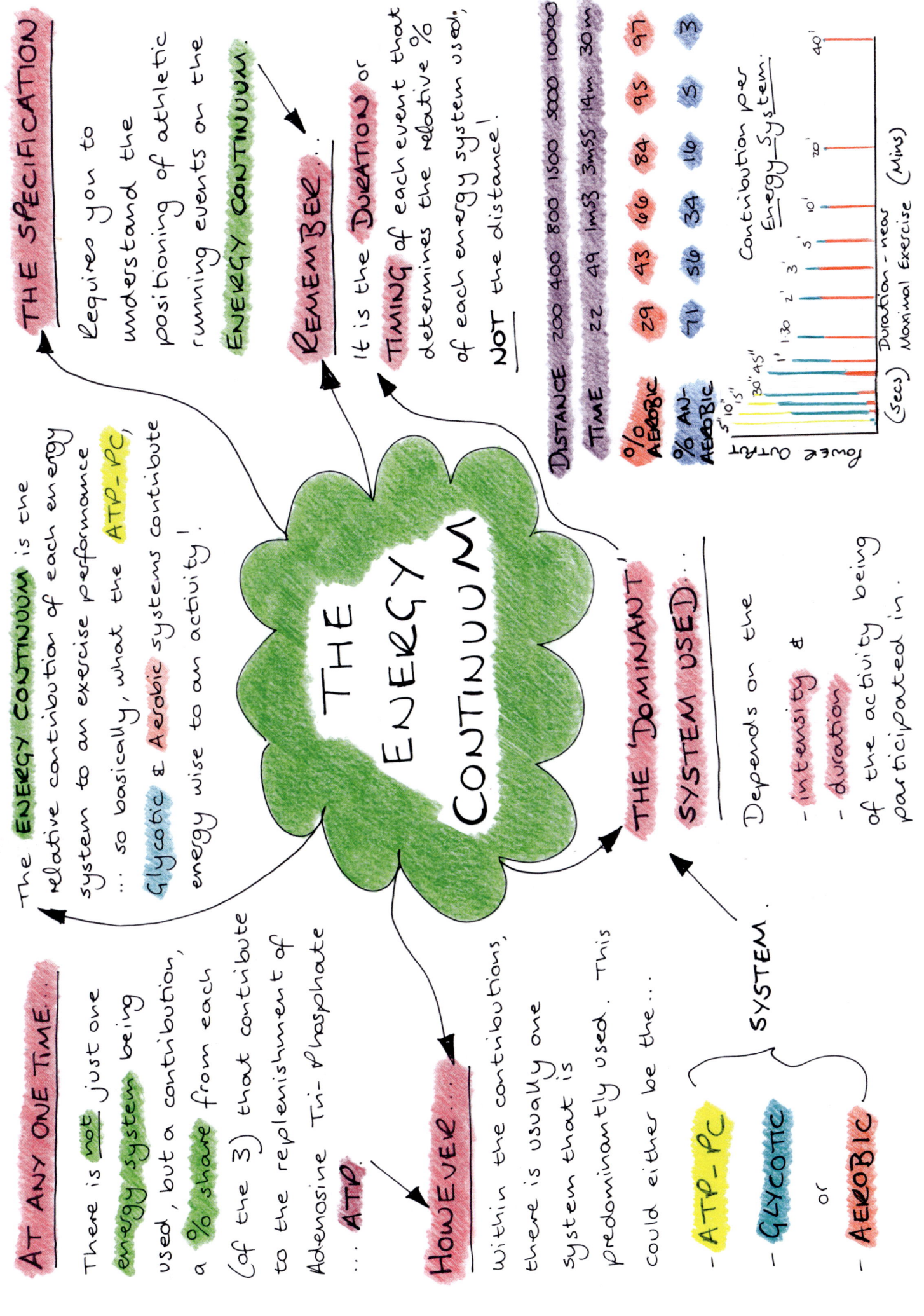

Contribution per Energy-System.

Power Output — (y axis)

Duration - near Maximal Exercise (Mins)
(secs)

5" 10" 15" 30" 45" 1' 1'30 2' 3' 5' 10' 20' 40'

The **ENERGY CONTINUUM** is the relative contribution of each energy system to an exercise performance ... so basically, what the **ATP-PC**, **Glycotic** & **Aerobic** systems contribute energy wise to an activity!

THE ENERGY CONTINUUM

AT ANY ONE TIME...

There is **not** just one energy system being used, but a contribution, a % share from each (of the 3) that contribute to the replenishment of Adenosine Tri-Phosphate ... ATP.

HOWEVER...

Within the contributions, there is usually one system that is predominantly used. This could either be the...

SYSTEM.

- ATP-PC
- GLYCOTIC
or
- AEROBIC

THE 'DOMINANT' SYSTEM USED...

Depends on the
- intensity &
- duration
of the activity being participated in.

53

ENERGY DEPLETION

PC STORES

- PC stores are needed to help replenish ATP molecules.

- If PC stores cannot be maintained, then the replenishment of ATP cannot occur quickly enough & so the intensity of exercise decreases.

- Increased P_i substantially impairs myofibrillar performance, decreases sarcoplasmic reticulum ($Ca2+$) release & contributes to the decreased activation.

GLYCOGEN

- Glycogen oxidation is a major source for ATP regeneration during prolonged exercise & high intensity exercise.

- It is also important because it contributes to the maintenance of oxidative metabolism (aerobic pathway & the breakdown of fats).

- Low muscle glycogen is associated with impaired sarcoplasmic reticulum ($Ca2+$) release & $Na+/K+$ pump function.

MUSCULAR FATIGUE...

- is defined as 'the inability to maintain power output during repeated muscular contractions'.

Factors that contribute to fatigue include...

FATIGUE

DEHYDRATION

- May cause a decrease in blood volume, skin blood flow, sweat rate, heat dissipation & an increase in core temperature & glycogen use.

- Reduces plasma volume & so increases blood viscosity, blood flow is reduced to muscles & the heart. Less blood into the heart in diastole, decreases amount that leaves in systole, causing $\dot{Q}$ to decrease.

- Sweat (= 2% of body weight can cause noticeable decrease of mental/physical performance. 5% loss = 30% decrease.

BUILD UP OF WASTE PRODUCTS

(Metabolic accumulation).

- During anaerobic exercise, CO_2 builds up in the blood & muscles, creating a hypoxic environment. the body cannot fulfil the O_2 delivery needs.

- which leads to an increase in lactic acid - dissociates into lactate & $H+$. As $H+$ levels increase, blood becomes more acidic (pH reduces). This stimulates free nerve endings in the muscle & lead to 'perception of pain'.

- The increase in $H+$ thought to be biggest indicator of fatigue as can...

- Inhibit the strength of action potential reaching myofibril by reducing concentration of $Na+$ influx & $K+$ efflux.

- Reduce $Ca2+$ released from sarcoplasmic reticulum.

- Inhibit $Ca2+$ binding to troponin, affecting muscle contractions.

Lactic acid is not the bad performance inhibitor. It is another fuel source (slow component of recovery).

The pain associated with post exercise was thought to be associated with lactic acid pooling. It is however to do with tiny muscle micro tears (DOMS)

54

FAST COMPONENT

- The fast component (or fast alactacid component) is the first stage of EPOC.

- The 2 main aspects of the fast component of EPOC are...

- Re-phosphorylation or replenishment of PC stores (the recovery time for PC stores are shown in the table below).

- Resaturation of oxymyoglobin & oxyhaemoglobin stores.

Muscle phosphagen restored (%)	Recovery time (secs)
10	10
50	30
75	60
87	90
93	120
97	150
99	180
101	210
102	240

Can be divided into 2

- the FAST component of recovery.
- the SLOW component of recovery.
- & the link with EPOC recovery rates

STAGES OF RECOVERY

EPOC - what is that?

Excess Post Oxygen Consumption... also known simply as Oxygen Debt.

It is the amount of O_2 that the body consumes following a period of exercise that is in excess of the pre-exercise oxygen consumption baseline level. The body will expend more calories during recovery from exercise than prior to exercise commencing.

The rise/increase in O_2 consumption post exercise is needed to resynthesise ATP used & to remove/resynthesise lactate

When looking at EPOC, need to consider...

- FAST
- SLOW

components.

Fast will be developed further here, slow on the next page.

GRAPH SHOWING EPOC PROCESSES

E- O_2 deficit.
C- O_2 use/consumption when exercising.
A - Alactic debt/EPOC fast replenishment component
D - Lactacid debt/EPOC slow replenishment component.
B- O_2 consumption at rest.

Graph: VO_2 L/min (4, 3, 2, 1, 0) vs recovery period (mins) (4, 8, 12, 16)
last exercise / rest exercise

STAGES OF RECOVERY II

REPLENISHMENT OF ENERGY STORES & the TWO HOUR WINDOW OF OPPORTUNITY

Post match, or post exercise meal to contain complex carbohydrates (CHO) & protein to increase muscle & liver glycogen stores & reduce the effects of muscle micro-tears, speeding up protein & glycogen resynthesis.

THE 48 HOUR WINDOW OF OPPORTUNITY

Allows performers to reduce the effects of Exercise Induced Muscle Damage (EIMD). During this period, muscle protein synthesis increases & protein breakdown increases dramatically. Studies show protein synthesis is stimulated & protein breakdown is suppressed when there is an increase in protein intake (post exercise). This, in turn, should reduce EIMD effects (usually as a result of 'new' exercises or excessive eccentric movements) Less damage = reduction in Doms (delayed onset of muscular soreness).

The second stage of recovery focusses on the SLOW component.

There are more factors to consider than the FAST component, but they are all here!

REHYDRATION

H_2O & electrolyte replacement.

PHYSICAL COOLING & THERMOREGULATION

Elevated temperature can remain for several hours, therefore a cool-down is important to return the body back to homeostasis (as quickly as possible).

SLOW COMPONENT

Everything after the replenishment of PC & oxymyoglobin stores (roughly 3 minutes) is categorised as part of the slow component.

This accounts for approximately 90% of EPOC. Resaturation of myglobin occurs here.

The aspects of the slow component of recovery are more time consuming / take longer & include...

OXIDATION OF LACTATE

The removal of lactate & H+. Approximately 65% of lactic acid is converted into CO_2 & H_2O. Another 20% turns into glycogen, 10% into protein & 5% into glucose.

WARMING UP & PRIMING

PRIMING EXERCISE

- A prior bout of high intensity exercise before a high intensity sporting activity to accelerate O₂ uptake, maximising the use of the aerobic system & activating this as the main pathway (as it is the most efficient).

- It is a way of manipulating the warm up to accentuate the benefits of utilising the aerobic system & so less reliance on the anaerobic systems & any issues associated with H+ build up/accumulation leading to fatigue. The neuromuscular system is also activated as more muscle fibres are recruited, reducing localised fatigue.

- Priming exercise is a method of increasing the rate of O₂ delivery in response to the demands of the exercise.

How do the energy systems...

- ATP-PC
- Glycotic
- Aerobic

respond acutely to the stress of...

3 important factors include...

- Intensity of exercise - Just below or above the intensity level of performance = intensity of performance

- The gap between the end of the priming exercise, & the start of performance (ideally between 10-20 minutes).

WARM UP

The benefits of a warm up include...

- Prepares the body for exercise effort.

- Increases body temperature, which in turn warms the muscles & enables better/more effective ATP conversion.

- Increases HR & Q

- Increase in volume of air breathed (in & out) per minute

- Capillaries dilate with oxygenated blood & vascular shunting.

- Better blood flow (slight) due to lower blood viscosity at higher temperature.

- Increase in blood pressure forces blood through arteries.

- Stretching of relevant joints & muscles prepares for full range of movement (ROM).

- Secretion of adrenaline increases metabolic rate.

57

1.4: Energy Systems

1. **Describe** the following forms of energy:

   a. Electrical   (1 mark)

   b. Potential   (1 mark)

   c. Chemical   (1 mark)

2. **Identify** the net ATP yield and main energy source for each energy system.

   (6 marks)

Energy Pathway	ATP Yield	Main Energy Source
ATP-PC System		
Anaerobic Glycolysis System		
Aerobic System		

3. Describe how ATP is replenished in the PC system. (3 marks)

4. State the main determinant of where track athletic events are placed on the energy continuum. (1 mark)

5. Suggest six possible physiological causes of muscle fatigue. (6 marks)

6. Summarise the benefits of priming on performance. (2 marks)

7. Explain the process of the fast component of the recovery. (4 marks)

8. Explain how the slow component of recovery is achieved. (6 marks)

9. Assess the relative contribution of the three energy systems on an 800m runner. (8 marks)

Total marks for 1.4: Energy systems: /39

2.1: Diet and nutrition and their effect on physical activity and performance

What you need to learn.	Yes	Nearly	No
2.1.1: Knowledge and understanding of dietary manipulation for performance pre-, during and post-physical activity.			
2.1.2: Optimal weight for performance to include energy balance, energy intake and expenditure.			
2.1.3: Electrolytes, hypotonic, hypertonic and isotonic solutions and their importance in maintaining hydration and performance.			
2.1.4: The role and use of supplementation to enhance energy stores, hydration, recovery, metabolic process and delay fatigue.			
2.1.5: Contemporary supplements.			
2.1.6: Strategies for ensuring optimal food, fuel and fluid intake for pre-, during and post-physical activity: carbohydrate (CHO) loading, two-hour window of opportunity, protein intake, pre-, during and post-event hydration.			

DURING PERFORMANCE

- Hydration & staying hydrated is key. Low level H_2O can lead to a decrease in blood plasma & increase in glycogen breakdown.
- This causes an increase in fatigue & core body temperature.
- Need to consume H_2O, electrolyte solutions & high GI CHO food stuffs.

POST PERFORMANCE

- Importantly there are 2 windows

1st Window — consume high GI CHO foods within the first 30 mins to enhance post exercise refuelling of muscle glycogen.
- Maintain hydration & electrolyte balance. This allows blood plasma levels to gradually return to normal, reducing blood viscosity & increases transport of vital nutrients for recovery.

2nd Window — consume CHO within the first 2 hrs to increase recovery rate. This speeds up the replenishment of glycogen stores.
- Protein should also be included to help speed up the recovery from micro tears. This is particularly important for high intensity/strength & power based performers.

DIETARY MANIPULATION

Must focus on...
- Pre-competition
- During performance
- Post performance

What is done to optimise performance & boost/aid recovery?

Can cause bloating & weight gain, so practise in training.

PRE-COMPETITION

- Increase carbohydrate intake (CHO).
- Eat low glycemic index (GI) meal 2-4 hrs prior to competition. Why? To maximise muscle & liver glycogen stores.
- Decrease fat & protein intake.
- Increase CHO an hour before can decrease glycogen stores.
- Increase GI CHO just prior to exercise/activity can be beneficial (high GI CHO).
- suitable for endurance & games based performers

CARBOHYDRATE LOADING

- A method that is used prior to exercise/performance, leading up to an event to maximise glycogen stores. Usually a 10 day programme.
- High intense training for 6-7 days prior to event to deplete glycogen stores.
- Diet high in fat & protein initially & low in CHO.
- Increase CHO intake 3-4 days prior to competition as well as tapering training intensity & levels of fat & protein intake.
- Result → high levels of loading & storage of muscle & liver glycogen stores. eg marathon.
- Assists with endurance based events.

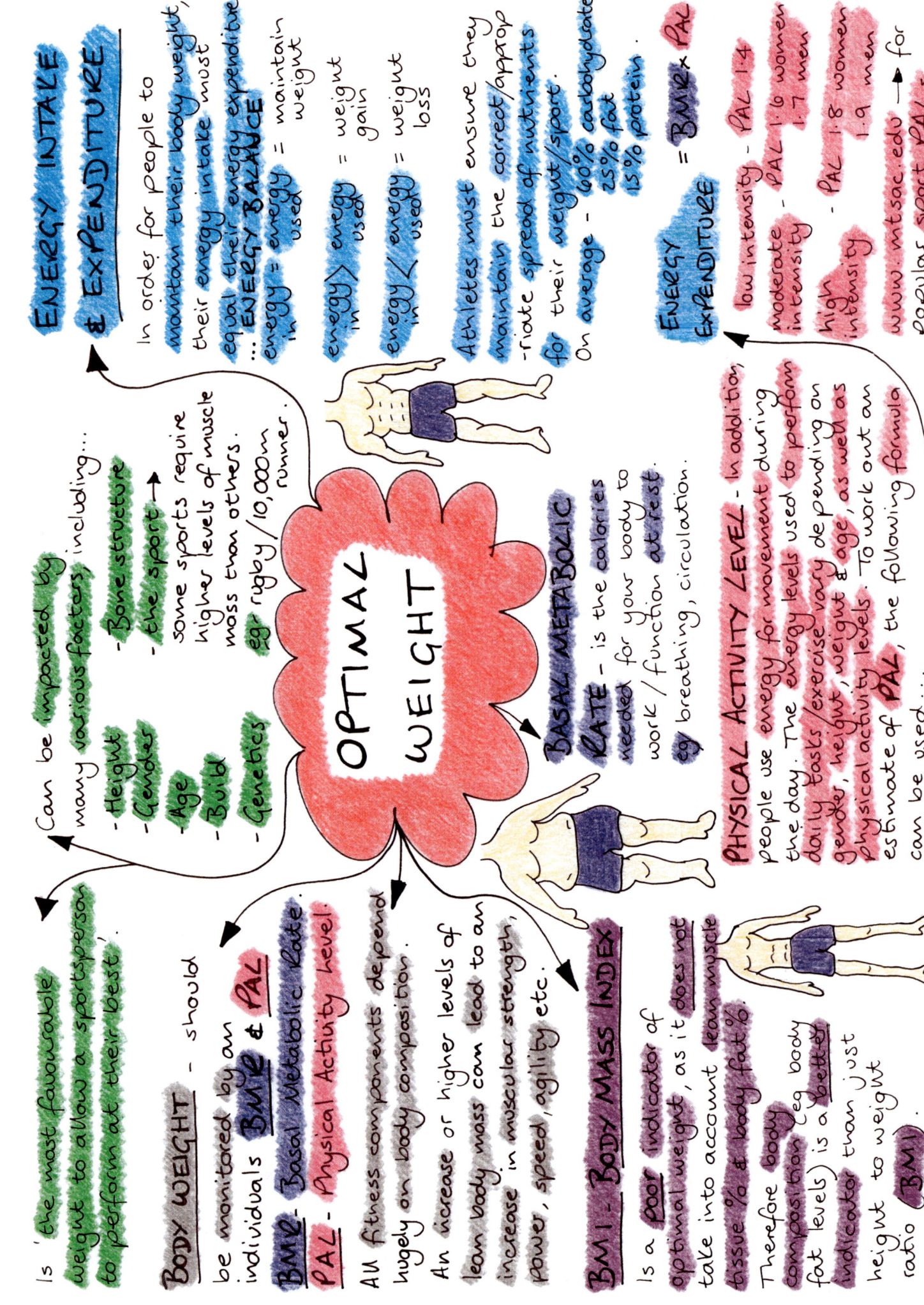

ENERGY INTAKE & EXPENDITURE

In order for people to maintain their body weight, their energy intake must equal their energy expenditure ... ENERGY BALANCE

energy = energy = maintain
in   used   weight

energy > energy = weight
in   used   gain

energy < energy = weight
in   used   loss

Athletes must ensure they maintain the correct/approp -riate spread of nutrients for their weight/sport.

On average - 60% carbohydrate
              25% fat
              15% protein.

ENERGY EXPENDITURE

= BMR × PAL

low intensity - PAL 1.4

moderate - PAL 1.6 women
intensity   1.7 men

high - PAL 1.8 women
intensity   1.9 men

www.mtsac.edu → for popular sport PALs

Can be impacted by many various factors including...

- Bone structure → - the sport
  - some sports require higher levels of muscle mass than others.
  - eg. rugby/10,000m runner.

- Height
- Genetics
- Age
- Build
- Genetics

OPTIMAL WEIGHT

BASAL METABOLIC RATE

- is the calories needed for your body to work / function at rest. eg. breathing, circulation.

PHYSICAL ACTIVITY LEVEL

- In addition, people use energy for movement during the day. The energy levels used to perform daily tasks/exercise vary depending on gender, height, weight & age, as well as physical activity levels. To work out an estimate of PAL, the following formula can be used ....

Is the most favourable weight to allow a sportsperson to perform at their best.

BODY WEIGHT

- should be monitored by an individuals BMR & PAL

BMR - Basal Metabolic Rate.

PAL - Physical Activity level.

All fitness components depend hugely on body composition.

An increase or higher levels of lean body mass can lead to an increase in muscular strength, power, speed, agility etc.

BMI - BODY MASS INDEX

Is a POOR indicator of optimal weight, as it does not take into account lean muscle tissue % & body fat %

Therefore body composition (eg. body fat levels) is a better indicator than just height to weight ratio (BMI).

62

ELECTROLYTE SOLUTIONS

HYPERTONIC

Have a higher osmolality than the body (more than 10% CHO). It supplements CHO or used post exercise, especially when the activity is high intensity or long duration. Should be consumed/taken with HYPOTONIC solutions to reduce dehydration levels.
eg marathon runner.

ISOTONIC

Have a similar osmolality as the body (6-8% CHO). These drinks quickly replace lost fluids & glucose.
Most sports drinks are isotonic.
eg Lucozade Sport, Powerade & Gatorade.
They are the preferred solution during exercise, sport or game.
eg football, netball, rugby.

OSMOLALITY

Refers to the concentration of dissolved particles of chemicals & minerals/electrolytes (eg Mg++) in a fluid.
Higher osmolality means more particles in the fluid (hypertonic), & lower osmolality means they are more diluted (hypotonic).

HYPOTONIC

Lower osmolality than the body (2-4% CHO)
Quickly replaces fluids & less CHO replacement.
Good for short duration activities. eg gymnastics & sprinting.

ELECTROLYTES

Are minerals that dissolve in a fluid creating positive or negative ions used in various metabolic roles/processes.

They are important for proper nerve & muscle function, maintaining pH levels & hydration

Electrolytes are lost through perspiration (sweating)

Examples of electrolytes essential for muscle contractions in the body are;

- SODIUM (Na+) involved in muscle excitability & cellular permeability.

- POTASSIUM (K+) involved in protein & CHO synthesis.

- CALCIUM (Ca++ or Ca2+) involved in muscle contraction within myofibril.

- MAGNESIUM (Mg++) involved in the proper functioning of the Na+/K+ - ATPase pump & helps maintain Ca++ homeostasis.

Plus... CHLORIDE, PHOSPHATE & BICARBONATE.

63

SUPPLEMENTS

BEETROOT JUICE

Drinking beetroot juice raises nitric oxide levels in the blood. This helps to promote vasodilation of blood vessels, leading to increased blood flow & O_2 to working muscles.

It also decreases the effects of DOMS & so is used post performance.

CAFFEINE

Is a stimulant. Increases mental alertness. It increases the breakdown of fat stores for energy, therefore decreasing the use of glycogen stores. Reduces fatigue for aerobic events (eg. marathon). However, excess caffeine can act as a diuretic & increase dehydration. Can also increase anxiety levels.

CREATINE MONOHYDRATE

'Creatine loading' is used to increase the PC stores in the muscles, thereby enhancing the replenishment of ATP.

This in turn helps to decrease recovery time & allows performers to participate in high intensity sports with greater levels of force & intensity eg power based sports, including; sprinting, rugby, weightlifting, & basketball.

This procedure can/could potentially lead to bloating, water retention & long term kidney damage, though the evidence is inconclusive.

CHERRY JUICE

Tart cherry juice has an antioxidant & anti-inflammatory properties.

It can decrease pain & accelerates recovery after exercise. Useful for both strength & endurance events.

APPLE JUICE

Contains Na, K & vinegar, however it is not used to replace electrolytes. Triggers a reflex in the mouth that sends a signal to the muscles to decrease cramp. Good for hot & humid conditions. Tastes horrible! though can decrease cramps by 40-45% faster than water!

VITAMIN D

Commonly known to be vital in absorbing dietary calcium to maintain bone health.

Increasing suggestions that vitamin D deficiency could negatively affect performance, ie muscular strength & endurance. Some elite clubs now encourage vitamin D supplementation & testing during the winter *Caution*

SODIUM BICARBONATE

Buffers the build up of lactate & H+, reducing blood acidity.

Allows the performer to work at a higher level of intensity, for longer without suffering the effects of fatigue. Can cause stomach cramps & nausea. eg 400m sprinter (runner).

* It is recommended that centres keep up-to-date with the use of contemporary supplements, as this is a dynamic aspect of sport science.

2.1: Diet and nutrition and their effect on physical activity and performance

1. **Explain** how an endurance athlete can manipulate their diet in preparation for an event. (6 marks)

2. **Define** the following terms:

   a. Optimum weight (1 mark)

   b. Energy balance (1 mark)

3. **Explain**, using two different scenarios when sports performers would want to create a positive and negative energy balance (4 marks)

4. **Compare** the practical use of all three electrolyte solutions. (6 marks)

5. **Analyse** the benefits of taking supplements in preparation and for recovery from physical activity. (8 marks)

6. **Examine** the post exercise dietary strategies that can be used to assist with the recovery process. (8 marks)

Total marks for 2.1: Diet and Nutrition: /34

2.2: Preparation and training methods in relation to maintaining and improving physical activity and performance

What you need to learn.	Yes	Nearly	No
2.2.1: Knowledge and understanding of preparation and training methods in relation to maintaining and improving physical activity and performance.			
2.2.2: Fitness tests: functional thresholds, lactate threshold/anaerobic threshold/maximum steady state, gas analysis, multi-stage fitness test, step tests, yo-yo test, Cooper minute run, Wingate test, maximum accumulated oxygen deficit (MAOD), RAST (repeat anaerobic sprint test), Cunningham and Faulkner, jump tests, Margaria-Kalaman, strength tests, agility tests, sprint tests < 100m.			
2.2.3: Interpret, calculate and present data (tables and graphs) based on fitness test results.			
2.2.4: Determinants of movement/running performance and their application to sprint, endurance and intermittent activities.			
2.2.5: Components of fitness: localised muscular endurance, VO2 max, anaerobic capacity, maximal strength, strength, power, speed, agility, coordination, reaction time, balance, flexibility, exercise economy, maximal and submaximal aerobic fitness.			
2.2.6: Principles of training: individual needs, specificity, progressive overload, Frequency Intensity Time and Type (FITT), overtraining, reversibility.			
2.2.7: Different ways of measuring and calculating intensity: percentage of functional intensity, percentage of one repetition maximum (RM), Rate of Perceived Exertion (RPE), percentage of functional threshold, target HR, work to rest ratios.			

2.2.8: Target heart rate: understanding use of Karvonens theory.			
2.2.9: Contemporary technologies used by the performer and coach to monitor fitness and performance.			
2.2.10: Periodisation: Macro, Meso and Micro Cycles, Knowledge and understanding of the preparation phase (general and specific), competition phase and transition phase.			
2.2.11: Methods of training and their appropriateness for different activities: interval, circuits, cross, continuous, fartlek, flexibility (static, ballistic and proprioceptive neuromuscular facilitation (PNF)), weights (free weights and machines), resistance (including pulleys, parachutes), assisted (including bungees, downhill), plyometrics, speed agility quickness (SAQ) and functional stability. Advantages and disadvantages of each method of training.			
2.2.12: Preparation for performance at altitude, in heat and humidity.			
2.2.13: Knowledge and understanding of strategies for speeding up recovery following physical activity: cooling down, massage, ice baths, compression clothing.			

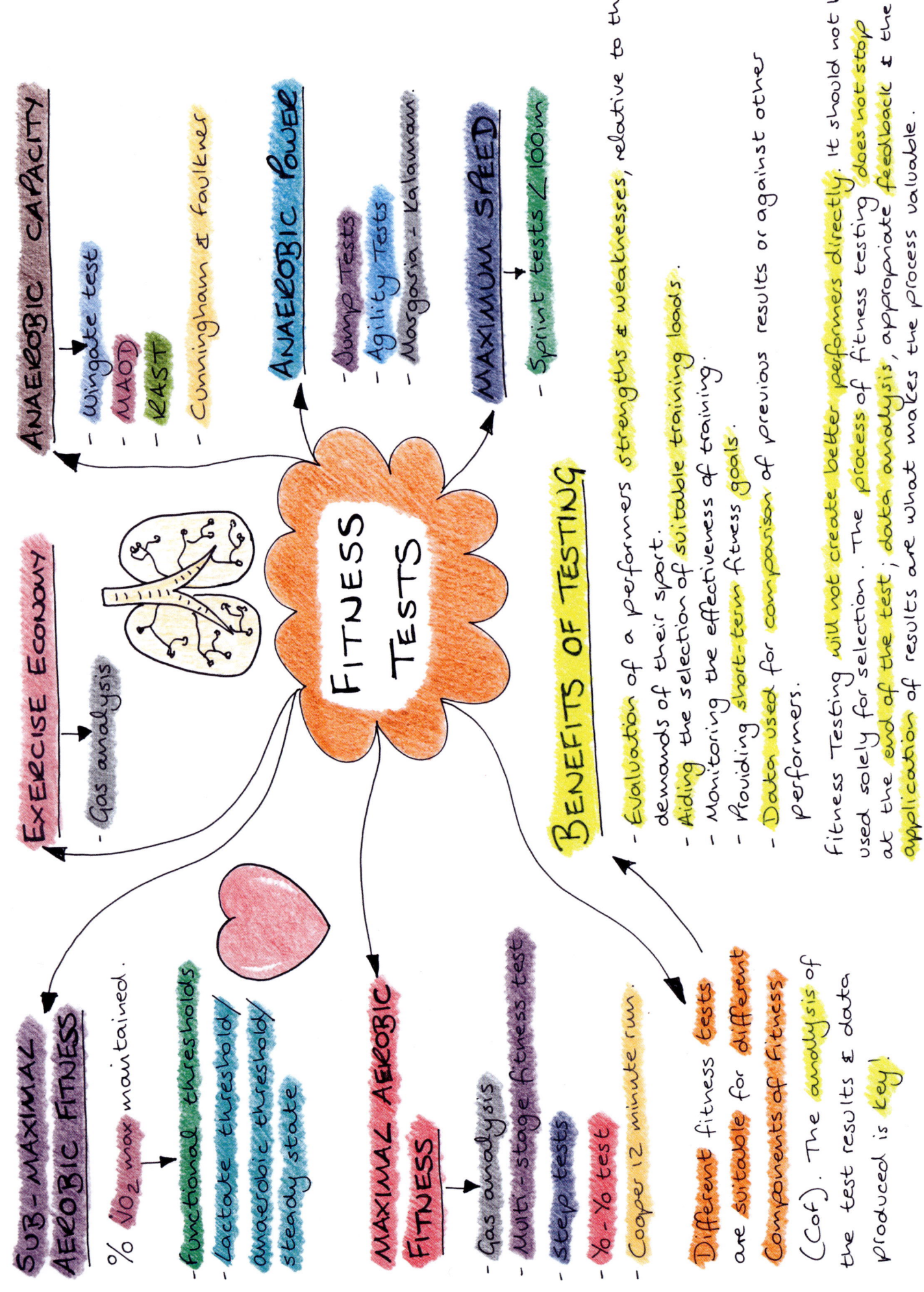

FITNESS TESTS

ANAEROBIC CAPACITY
- Wingate test
- MAOD
- RAST
- Cunningham & Faulkner

ANAEROBIC POWER
- Jump Tests
- Agility Tests
- Margaria - Kalamann

MAXIMUM SPEED
- Sprint tests < 100m

EXERCISE ECONOMY
- Gas analysis

SUB-MAXIMAL AEROBIC FITNESS
% VO₂ max maintained.
- Functional thresholds
- Lactate threshold/
- Anaerobic threshold/ steady state

MAXIMAL AEROBIC FITNESS
- Gas analysis
- Multi-stage fitness test
- Step tests
- Yo-Yo test
- Cooper 12 minute run

Different fitness tests are suitable for different components of fitness

BENEFITS OF TESTING
- Evaluation of a performers strengths & weaknesses, relative to the demands of their sport.
- Aiding the selection of suitable training loads.
- Monitoring the effectiveness of training.
- Providing short-term fitness goals.
- Data used for comparison of previous results or against other performers.

Fitness Testing will not create better performes directly. It should not be used solely for selection. The process of fitness testing does not stop at the end of the test; data analysis, appropriate feedback & the application of results are what makes the process valuable.

(CofA). The analysis of the test results & data produced is key!

68

FITNESS TESTS: AEROBIC

LACTATE THRESHOLD/ ANAEROBIC THRESHOLD/ MAXIMUM STEADY STATE

- Laboratory test where the velocity or resistance on a treadmill, bike or rowing ergometer is increased at regular intervals (every min).
- Blood samples are taken at each increment (to measure lactate levels (mmol/L)).
- Usually test $\dot{V}O_2$ max, data, CO_2 levels & RPE also measured.

YO-YO TEST

- Athlete starts running 20m & then turns & returns to starting point on the bleep.
- There is an active recovery period of 10 secs between each shuttle (there/back). Must walk/jog to other cone & back (5m distance)

FUNCTIONAL THRESHOLDS

- Most common test is to find the highest average power you can sustain for an hour. (watts)
- This is often used to determine training zones when using a power meter & to measure improvement.
- Using a wattbike, you have to maintain the same pace for 20mins. Average power & heart rate recorded at the end of the test.

GAS ANALYSIS

- A laboratory test where velocity or resistance on a treadmill, bike or rowing ergometer is increased regularly (usually at minute intervals).
- Oxygen uptake is calculated from measured ventilation & the O_2 & CO_2 in the expired air. The maximal level is deter-mined at/near test completion. (plateauing of O_2 uptake).

MULTI-STAGE FITNESS TEST

- The test requires the performer to run 20m in time with a bleep on a pre-recording.
- One foot must be placed on/beyond the 20m marker at end of shuttle.
- Fail to get there-warning given. Run twice 2 or 3 then have to finish. exhaustion.

STEP TESTS

- Step up/down on the platform at rate of 30 steps per min for 5 mins. Performer then immediately sits down after completion & heart beats counted between 60-90, 120-150 & 180-210 secs. after finishing.
- Fitness index (100 x test duration (secs)) ÷ (2 x sum of heart beats in the recovery periods)

COOPER 12 MINUTE RUN

- The test requires the performer to run the greatest distance they can in 12 minutes. Usually/best completed on 400m track but any accurately measured area is fine.

FITNESS TESTS: ANAEROBIC

MARGARIA - KALAMAN

- Start 6m in front of the first step, then sprint to & up the flight of steps, taking 3 steps at a time. (3, 6, 9)
- Time taken to get from step 3-9 is recorded starting when the foot was first in contact with step 3 & stops when foot contacts step 9.

SPRINT TESTS / 100m

- Common - 30m sprint. More accurately measured when use timing gates.
- Speed tests modified with specific physiological requirements for an activity (differ for netball compared to football).
- More sport specific when below 100m, most well below this.

STRENGTH TESTS

- Common tests 1RM or 3RM using compound or multi-joint exercises (squat, bench press, deadlift, powerclean).
- Other tests - isokinetic strength test & hand grip dynamometer.

JUMP TESTS

- Tests used include the broad jump (standing long jump), vertical jump (sargent jump) or more commonly the counter-movement jump. (CMJ)
- Can be measured manually, via use of force plates or timing mats.

AGILITY TESTS

- In the 505 agility test, athlete runs 15m, turns on line & runs back through 5m marker.
- Time recorded when the athlete first runs through the 5m marker & stopped when return through marker (time taken to cover 5m up & back distance - 10m in total).
- Other popular tests - Balson agility, T test & Illinois agility.

WINGATE TEST

- The athlete performs this on a cycle ergometer where he/she pedals as fast as possible with no resistance for 30 secs. Revolutions are recorded for each 5 sec intervals to work out power output

MAXIMUM ACCUMULATED OXYGEN DEFICIT (MAOD)

- The measurement of O2 deficit is done by calculating the difference between total O2 required & consumed.
(amount of energy provided by the anaerobic system)
- Performed at a constant speed until point of exhaustion reached - run/cycle.

REPEAT ANAEROBIC SPRINT TEST (RAST)

- Athlete performs 35m maximal sprint.
- After 10 secs, repeat from opposite end of 35m track. Repeat for 6 sprints.
- Each 35m timed - work out power output & fatigue index

CUNNINGHAM & FAULKNER

- Treadmill is set to 8.0 mph (12.9 km/hr) & incline of 20%
- Run to exhaustion & time is recorded in seconds.

70

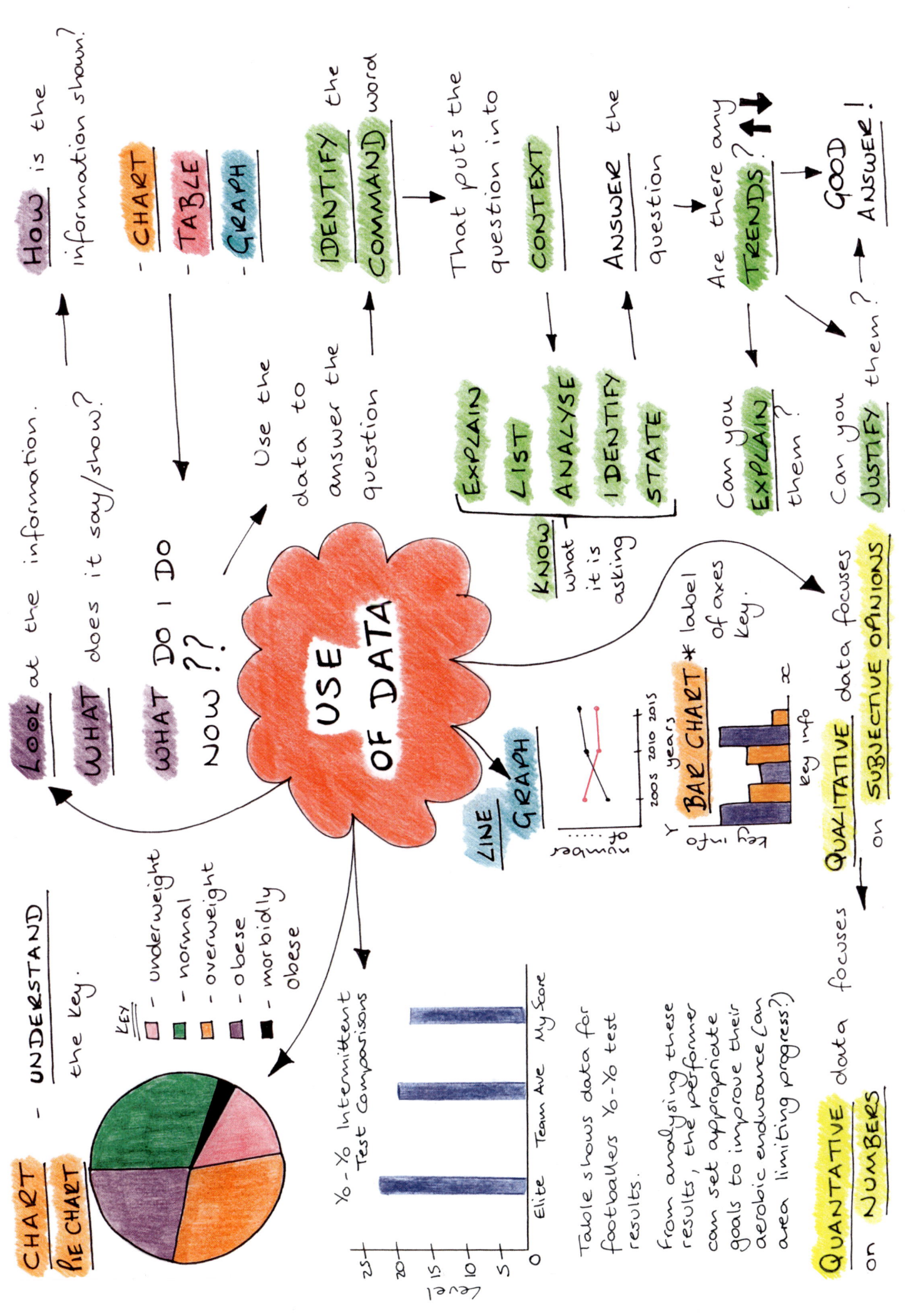

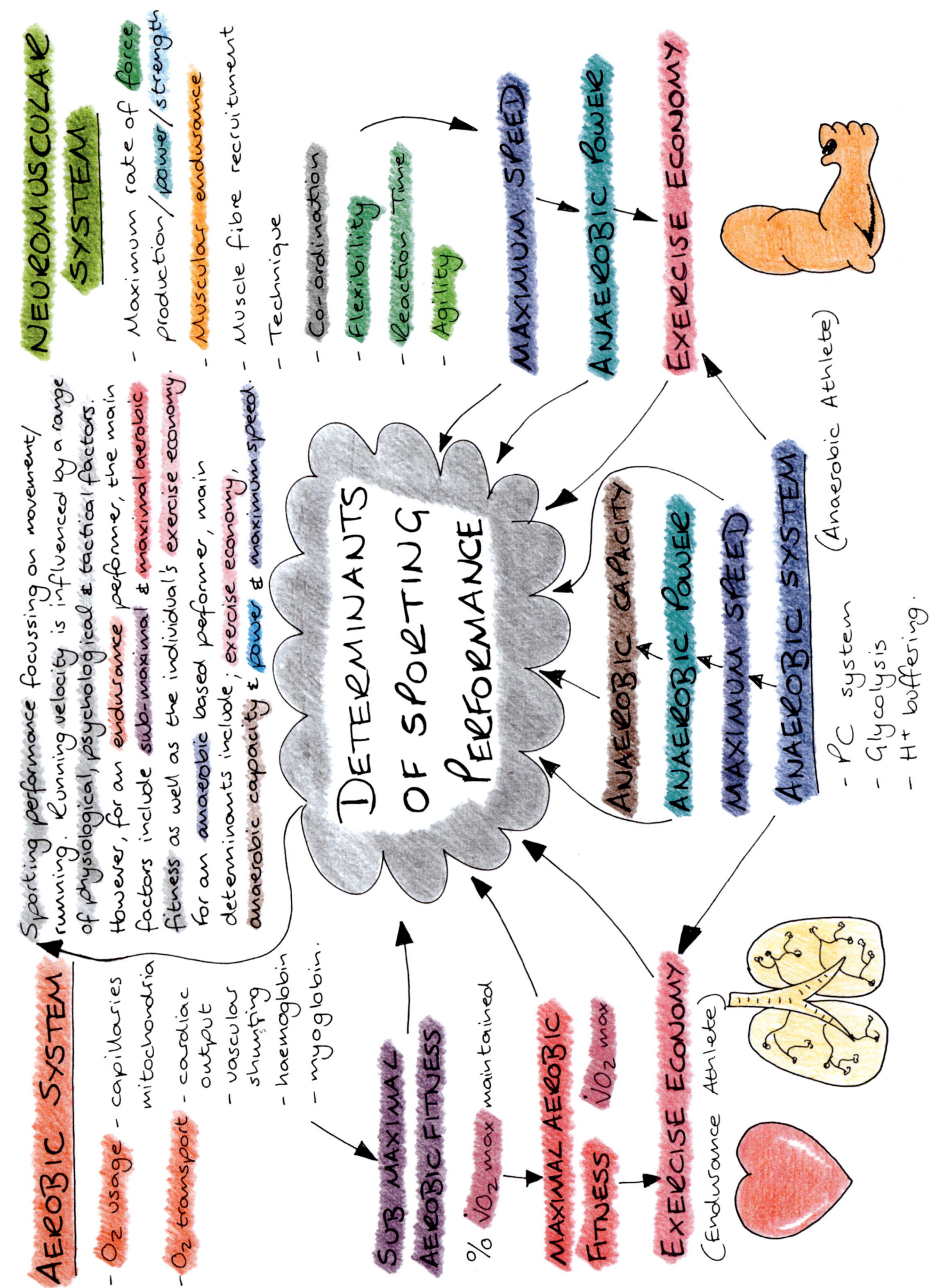

DETERMINANTS OF SPORTING PERFORMANCE

NEUROMUSCULAR SYSTEM
- Maximum rate of Force production / power/strength
- Muscular endurance
- Muscle fibre recruitment
- Technique
- Co-ordination
- Flexibility
- Reaction Time
- Agility

MAXIMUM SPEED → **ANAEROBIC POWER** → **EXERCISE ECONOMY**

Sporting performance focussing on movement/running. Running velocity is influenced by a range of physiological, psychological & tactical factors. However, for an endurance performer, the main factors include sub-maximal & maximal aerobic fitness as well as the individual's exercise economy. For an anaerobic based performer, main determinants include; exercise economy, anaerobic capacity & power & maximum speed.

AEROBIC SYSTEM
- O_2 usage - capillaries, mitochondria
- O_2 transport - cardiac output, vascular shunting, haemoglobin, myoglobin

SUB MAXIMAL AEROBIC FITNESS
% VO_2 max maintained

MAXIMAL AEROBIC FITNESS · VO_2 max

EXERCISE ECONOMY (Endurance Athlete)

ANAEROBIC SYSTEM (Anaerobic Athlete)
- PC system
- Glycolysis
- H+ buffering

ANAEROBIC CAPACITY
ANAEROBIC POWER
MAXIMUM SPEED

COMPONENTS OF FITNESS

can be split into 2 distinct categories...

- AEROBIC - this page.
- ANAEROBIC - next page.

COMPONENTS OF FITNESS - AEROBIC

MAXIMAL AEROBIC FITNESS

- Maximal aerobic fitness refers to the athletes ability to transport & utilise oxygen, measured by VO_2 max, the maximal amount of oxygen that can be used during intense exercise.

- eg endurance athletes - runners, swimmers & cyclists.

EXERCISE ECONOMY

- The economy of movement relates to the quantity of oxygen or energy required to move at a given speed/velocity or generate a specific amount of power.

- The economy of movement is influenced by the neuro-muscular co-ordination; % type I muscle fibres, elastic energy storage, joint stability & flexibility.

- determines performance as it is the ability to transfer energy → movement, so performance differs.

SUBMAXIMAL AEROBIC FITNESS

- Submaximal aerobic fitness is the ability to transport & utilise oxygen for a prolonged period of time, up to but never exceeding 85% of Maximum Heart Rate - MHR.

- eg endurance athletes again, run, swim, cycle.

LOCALISED MUSCULAR ENDURANCE

- Is the ability of certain muscles or muscle groups to perform repeated contractions against a submaximal resistance.

- eg- rock climbing requires high levels of muscular endurance in order to climb the route/crag.

VO_2 MAX

- Is the highest rate of oxygen consumption attainable during maximal or exhaustive exercise.

- As exercise intensity increases, so too does oxygen consumption. However, a point is reached where exercise intensity can continue to increase without the associated rise in oxygen consumption.

- eg endurance athletes such as marathon runners & triathletes have high VO_2 max levels.

CO-ORDINATION

- the ability to move 2 or more body parts under control, smoothly & efficiently either with movements or with external object (ball).
- Can be head/eye, eye, hand/eye, foot/eye.
- eg basketball - executing a lay up correctly (with multiple sub sequences).

REACTION TIME

- time between the presentation of a stimulus & the initiation of the muscular (response) to that stimulus (movement).
- eg swimming, 50m fly, reaction to the electronic starter gun.

BALANCE

- ability to retain centre of mass over base of support when moving (dynamic) or stationary (static)
- eg static - holding Crucifix in gymnastics, dynamic - dribbling in football while being tackled.

FLEXIBILITY

- the range of movement available at a joint.
- eg being flexible in dance aids performance by creating better movements & more fluid positions (splits).

AGILITY

- 'the ability to quickly & precisely move/change direction without losing balance or time.'
- Defn evolved, recently defined as 'rapid whole body movement with change of velocity and/or direction in response to stimulus'. Need quick reflexes, balance, speed & co-ordination.
- eg in rugby union - a winger to outwit opponents.

COMPONENTS OF FITNESS- ANAEROBIC

POWER

- the ability to exert a maximal force in as short a time as possible.
  power = strength × speed
- eg explosive power needed to maximise horizontal displacement in shot putt.

SPEED

- the maximum rate at which a performer is able to cover a distance or perform a movement in a chosen period of time (whole or past body)
- Speed = distance ÷ time
- eg 100m sprinter to finish race first.

ANAEROBIC CAPACITY

- is the total amount of energy obtainable from anaerobic energy systems (PC & anaerobic glycolysis) in a single bout of exercise.
- eg a 400m runner needs a high level of anaerobic capacity.

MAXIMAL STRENGTH

- is the greatest amount of force that a muscle/muscle groups can voluntarily produce during a single maximal contraction.
- eg weight/powerlifting - lifting maximum load.

STRENGTH

- is the maximal force produced in a muscle/muscle groups you can apply against a load or during a contraction.
- eg in rugby league when wrestling someone to the ground in a tackle.

PRINCIPLES OF TRAINING

SPECIFICITY

Focusses on the most appropriate way to develop the required Components of Fitness (CoF) for the sport/position.

Should be relevant to the sport/position & where possible match the activity.

Factors to consider include...
- contribution of energy systems, CoF, muscle fibre types, skills & movements required in the sport/position.

FITT
- FREQUENCY
- INTENSITY
- TIME
- TYPE

Classed as one even though separate sections. Both Specificity & Progressive Overload can be met by manipulating FITT

Frequency - 'how often' performer trains

Intensity - 'how hard'. Can be manipulated by changing length of session, increasing resistance, modify work/rest ratios. Should be specific to activity (training zones).

Time - 'how long' the length of session. Should be specific to aims & sport & can be adjusted by progressive overload.

Type - 'the method' the type of training should be specific to the aims & sport (matching), but will vary depending on the periodised training year.

OVERTRAINING

May occur when training too frequently with little/no recovery between sessions. Does not allow enough time for repair of micro tears or the replenishment of energy stores which could ultimately lead to fatigue, causing illness and/or injury.

INDIVIDUAL NEEDS

* Do not confuse this with Specificity *

Individual Needs focusses on the person/individual.

Specificity focusses on the sport/activity/position.

Factors that influence include:
Age, gender, weight, height, experience, previous injuries, strengths & weaknesses, current level of fitness & level of performance.

REVERSIBILITY

'Use it or lose it'. Adaptations gained through regular & progressive training will be lost if training at appropriate levels are not maintained.

This generally occurs if athletes are ill/injured for any period. For this reason, health & fitness experts are not in favour of 'total rest' & some form of optimal exercise' should be done in recovery phase.

PROGRESSIVE OVERLOAD

'More than normal', gradually working with more intensity throughout the training programme. This allows the body to adapt to incremental training demands, improving fitness levels safely & reducing the risk of injury.

Overload can be applied by increasing duration, intensity levels (% max HR, % 1RM, adjust work/rest ratio), more difficult exercises or increasing frequency.

75

MEASURING & CALCULATING INTENSITY

BORG SCALE
RATE OF PERCEIVED EXERTION - RPE

- Is a subjective measure of exertion based on a 6-20 scale, that provides an estimate of HR during physical activity - more accurate experienced performers.

- High correlation between a persons perceived exertion rating x10 & actual HR during physical activity. eg: exertion rating = 10
  $10 \times 10 = 100$ bpm (approx).

- The Borg Scale is used in lab tests & often preferred method of monitoring intensity for people with cardio-respiratory issues.

ratings:

6	
7	Very, very, very light
8	Very light
9	
10	Fairly light
11	
12	Somewhat hard
13	
14	Hard
15	
16	Very hard
17	
18	Very, very hard
19	Maximum exertion
20	

% OF FUNCTIONAL THRESHOLD

- Calculated by the HR that can be sustained for a 1 hour race effort. Used as a physiological marker where certain training zones can be established.

- A 30 minute full effort test is conducted, with the average HR for the last 20 mins used to determine the intensity of functional threshold.

TARGET HEART RATE

- The aerobic training zone is 60-80% MHR & anaerobic training zone above 80% MHR.

FORMULA

Target HR = ((MHR - resting HR) × % intensity) + RHR.

- Main issue with 220-age is that it does not allow for individual differences in RHR. Including heart rate reserve (MHR-RHR) into the equation allows a more accurate training zone to be determined.

WORK TO REST RATIOS

- Way of determining intensities for interval training

1:1 w/r means rest period inbetween exercise is the same as work period

1:2 w/r means inbetween exercise should be twice the length of work period

- high intensity, tolerate lactate, work at 2:1

- speed, need more rest, 1:4 or 1:5.

% OF 1 REP MAX

- Is the maximum amount of weight a performer can lift in a single repetition for a given exercise. It is usually performed using a compound or multi-joint exercise. eg: squat, bench press (barbell) or deadlift.

- Strength & conditioning coaches use % 1RM to manage training loads & intensities based on the aims of the programme.

% of 1 RM for strength training

strength endurance - 60-70%
hypertrophy - 70-85%
strength - 85-100%
power - 90-100%

Reps decrease from 13-20, 6-13
1-6 & 1-6 endurance → power

CONTEMPORARY TECHNOLOGIES

TRACKMAN

- The trackman machine is becoming increasingly popular in golf, where it can track a shot from 6 foot pitches to 400 yard drives.
- Pinpointing the landing position with an accuracy of less than 1 foot at 100 yards. The shots can be presented in 3D, illustrating the trajectory as well as other parameters in realtime (data can be delivered to electronic devices such as an iPad within a second).
- Examples of key parameters include ... swing technique, launch angle, smash factor, ball speed, club head speed, attack angle & club path.

ADIDAS GMR INSOLES

- This smart insole can track the players' running speed, the power of the kick, touch & control/distance run by the player & the ability to pass the football.
- It is motorised by a Jacquard chip (Google) placed inside the insole of the football boot.

FITNESS TRACKERS

- Heart rate monitors & pedometers are still used, though the evolution of fitness trackers & smart wrist bands have combined both & added extra data.
- These devices track the HR (though some have stopped this on newer versions to save battery) & also track distance, calories used, steps & monitor sleep.

GLOBAL POSITIONING SYSTEM - GPS

- Commonly used by elite athletes in team sports during matches & in training. The performance analyst uses the stats to feedback to the strength & conditioning coach. Stats included are ... metres covered, top sprint speed & heart rate data.
- Data is used to manage player workload & developing areas of weakness.
- Coaches are able to establish player physiological limitations & use the data for basis of making tactical changes during games as stats are now available concurrently.
- More affordable GPS units are now available & are being developed at a fast pace. These can be purchased via the use of a smart watch & can be used for various sports, both on land & in water.
  e.g. Skagen Falster 3.

BAT SENSOR

- Bat sensors (Intel-powered Specular or Stancebeam) can be placed at the top of the bat & can measure key elements such as ... back lift angle, follow through angle, impact angle, maximum bat speed, bat speed at impact, time to impact, 3D swing & plane path.
- Used to calculate shot timing efficiency & correlate data with HawkEye to see how effective the shot is & how it can be improved.

There are many! Examples here include ...

77

PERIODISATION

COMPETITION PHASE (B)

The aims of this phase are to maintain fitness & conditioning & focus on 'in-season' competition skills, tactics & strategies. The volume of training decreases, but intensity increases in an attempt to mimic game/activity intensity - clear link to specificity.

TRANSITION PHASE (C)

The main transition period is after the competition phase (off season) & athletes traditionally utilise cross-training methods here at a lower intensity to maintain a level of conditioning.

During a long season or when an athlete may have to peak more than once, the competition phase may be subdivided (transition period where training is tapered between mesocycles to allow for recovery from in-season fatigue and/or injury.)

Performance peak
Performance
Intensity
Sport form
A1 A2 B C

MACROCYCLE

There are numerous phases, including...

- The whole training year or training cycle that can be subdivided into **3** distinct phases.

- Preparatory Phase
- Competition Phase
- Transition Phase

Focusses on the systematic variation of training to allow athletes to peak at an optimal time or times during the competition phase or season.

It divides the training year into smaller, more manageable phases.

MESOCYCLE

The macrocycle is broken down/divided into various mesocycles - depending on activity & length of season. Focussed on specific areas eg- power, strength.

MICROCYCLE

Each mesocycle is broken down int a weekly microcycle. Led by the aim of mesocycle, though can focus on +/- in performance training.

PREPARATORY PHASE (A)

Part 1 - General Conditioning - high volume, low intensity to develop an endurance base. Prepare the body for further increases in intensity in future cycles.

Part 2 - Competition specific Training. Intensity gets progressively higher than in Part 1 with an increased focus on speed & strength training.

Greater focus on game techniques & tactics.

METHODS OF TRAINING - AEROBIC

FARTLEK
- Swedish for 'speed play' & a form of continuous exercise as there are no breaks.
- Involves changes in pace/speed and or gradient/terrain.
- Also similar to interval training as periods of high & low intensity.
- Variations in intensity allow both aerobic & anaerobic energy systems to be used.
- Develops aerobic fitness, muscular endurance & speed.
- Intensities can be manipulated to mimic the sport/activity training for.

Advantages - modified to mimic game intensity, develops numerous CoF

Disadvantages - difficult to track appropriate intensity level (unless monitored by coach/use wearable tech).

LEARN
- Key characteristics & +/- for each method of training listed.

CROSS
- Traditionally used in off season to maintain base level of physical conditioning by varying activities.

Advantages - allows body to recover, maintain conditioning, decreases risk of injury & decreases risk of burn out.

Disadvantages - may need extra kit/equipment, cost, non sport specific

CONTINUOUS
- sustained exercise performed at low to moderate intensity (60-80% of MHR) e.g run, swim, cycle.

Advantages - develops the aerobic system, minimal equipment needed, low risk of injury due to intensity levels & efficient for weight/fat loss.

Disadvantages - non sports specific (especially games), time consuming, can be boring!

CIRCUITS
- Involves a series of exercises performed at stations one after the other, with rest periods between each station.

Advantages - Use simple exercises, time efficient, can do full body workout, can focus on area(s) of weakness, can be general fitness based, or sport specific or skills based. Not much equipment needed (use body weight).

Disadvantages - can be too generic, not specialised enough, space.

INTERVAL
- Bouts of training with rest intervals between repetitions.
- Work/rest ratio can be adapted to target both aerobic & anaerobic systems (increase work period, lower intensity).

Advantages - W/R can be adapted to target specific energy systems, times that mimic competition, increases lactate/anaerobic threshold, rest allows PC replenishment.

Disadvantages - if intensity is too high, lead to early fatigue or overtraining.

METHODS OF TRAINING - ANAEROBIC

The full range of **Anaerobic** MoT will be discussed on pages. Again remember key points & +/- for each method listed

RESISTANCE

- This MoT is designed to improve maximal speed, start acceleration & speed endurance.

- As well as pulleys & parachutes, sledge towing (with weights) can also be used.

Advantages - helps to increase speed, acceleration, speed endurance & leg strength. Also adds variation to training.

Disadvantages - reduces ROM (range of movement) of leg action -eliminates part of eccentric phase with early knee extension - potential to minimise + effects on speed.

ASSISTED

- 'over speed' training where athlete attempts to run faster than normal, get used to faster cadence (+ 5-10%).

- Done by running downhill or pulled by bungee

Advantages - increases speed of neural pathways & excitability of muscle fibres (increase speed), adds variety to training.

Disadvantages - not normal 'running' action, timing unusual, affecting neuromuscular patterns involved. Increase in micro tears (eccentric).

WEIGHTS

FREE WEIGHTS & MACHINES

- Can be manipulated to improve **muscular strength**, **power** or **muscular endurance** & used to increase muscular hypertrophy.

- Recent studies show that regular **strength training** can **decrease** the risk of injury in sport.

- CoF developed is determined by the resistance, repetitions & sets performed & is usually monitored through % 1 RM.

(85%+ = strength, 75-85% hypertrophy, strength endurance 80-70%).

- Free weight exercises are performed using dumbbells, barbells and kettlebells, whereas machine weights involve the use of specialised **fitness machines** with weighted plates attached that work via a cam & pulley system.

Advantages - can be sports specific (more so with free weights), variation in single & multi-joint exercises, can focus on different CoF & adaptations (intensity dependant), can focus on specific muscle groups (more so with machines).

Disadvantages - may need a spotter to reduce injury risk (free weights), non-sports specific (machines), expensive (esp machines).

METHODS OF TRAINING – ANAEROBIC II

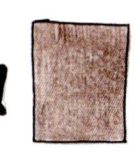

FUNCTIONAL STABILITY

- Refers to methods & strategies used in physiotherapy & rehabilitation in recovery from injury & performance enhancing training.

- Integrates mobility, strengthening & dynamic stabilisation.

- eg. using a wobble board to develop proprioception in recovery from an ankle injury, or performing resistance exercises using a gym/yoga ball.

Advantages - develops proprioception & dynamic balance, aids recovery & develops core muscle strength

Disadvantages - does not develop whole body strength, focusses on targetted muscle groups, nor lead to significant levels of muscular hypertrophy.

SPEED, AGILITY, QUICKNESS - SAQ

- eg. ladder drills, mini-hurdles & side stepping. Performed at speed in attempt to develop speed, agility & co-ordination

Advantages - variety of exercises & can be sports specific (esp. games).

Disadvantages - need specialist equipment.

PLYOMETRICS

- A method that is explosive & harnesses the elastic energy in the stretch shortening cycle (SSC).

- A form of interval training involving hopping, bounding & jumping (box jumps).

ECCENTRIC PHASE

Preloading the muscle group(s) as muscles are stretched.

AMORTISATION PHASE

(Transition) The time from the end of the eccentric phase to the initiation of the concentric muscle action (delay). If this phase lasts too long, the energy stored during the eccentric phase dissipates as heat & the stretch reflex will not increase muscle activity during the concentric phase.

CONCENTRIC PHASE

Energy stored during eccentric phase is either used to increase force of movement or is dissipated as heat. The stored elastic energy increases the force produced during the concentric phase.

Advantages - rapid power development, sports specific exercises can be used (eg high, long & triple jump).

Disadvantages - can increase risk of injury, longer recovery time due to stress during eccentric movement (increase in micro-tears). Exercises can be quite demanding & advanced, so difficult for beginners/novices.

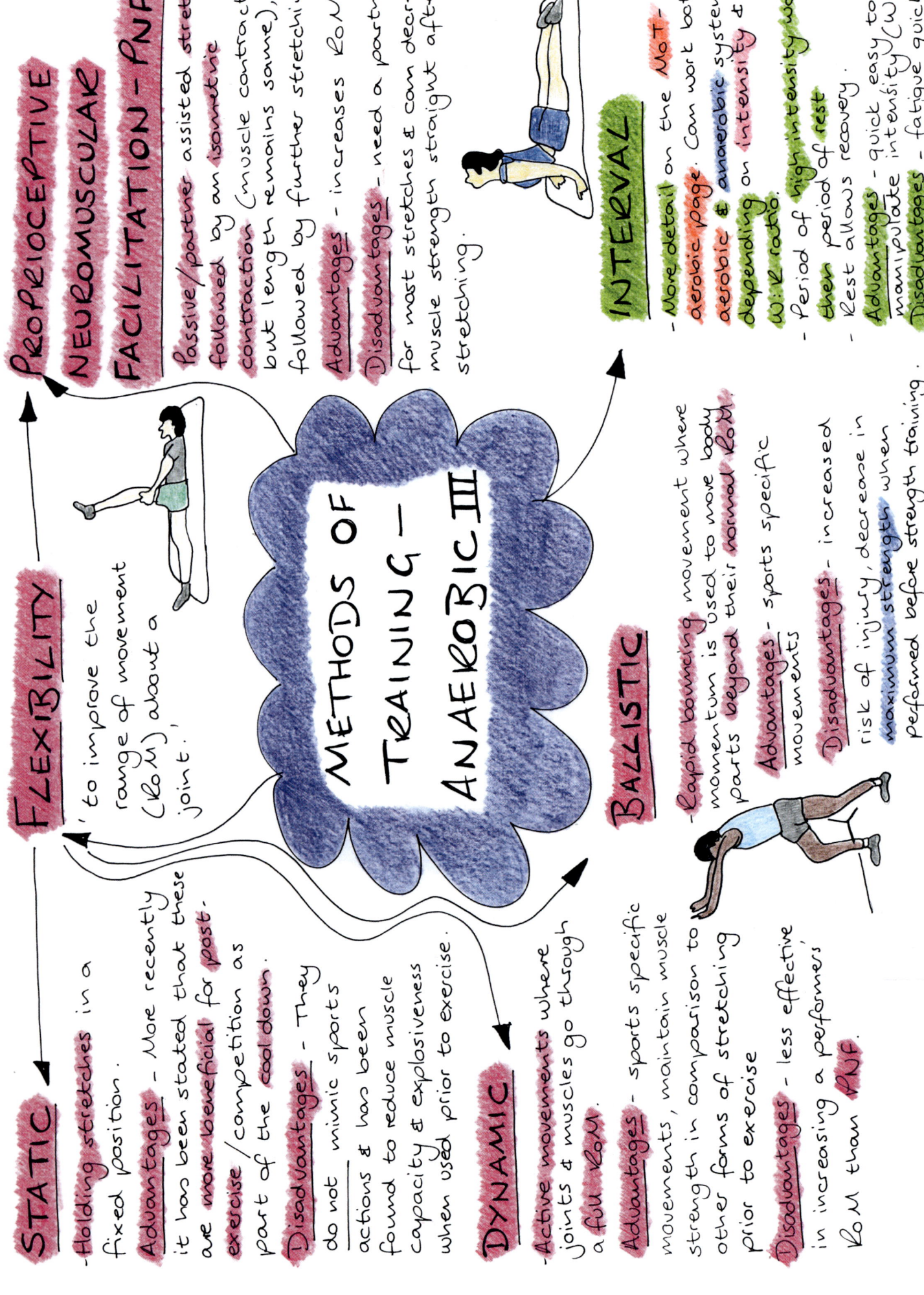

METHODS OF TRAINING — ANAEROBIC III

FLEXIBILITY

'to improve the range of movement (RoM) about a joint.'

PROPRIOCEPTIVE NEUROMUSCULAR FACILITATION - PNF

- Passive/partner assisted stretch, followed by an isometric contraction (muscle contracts but length remains same), followed by further stretching.

Advantages - increases RoM

Disadvantages - need a partner for most stretches & can decrease muscle strength straight after stretching.

STATIC

- Holding stretches in a fixed position.

Advantages - More recently it has been stated that these are more beneficial for post-exercise/competition as part of the cool down.

Disadvantages - They do not mimic sports actions & has been found to reduce muscle capacity & explosiveness when used prior to exercise.

DYNAMIC

- Active movements where joints & muscles go through a full RoM.

Advantages - sports specific movements, maintain muscle strength in comparison to other forms of stretching prior to exercise

Disadvantages - less effective in increasing a performers RoM than PNF.

BALLISTIC

- Rapid bouncing movement where momentum is used to move body parts beyond their normal RoM.

Advantages - sports specific movements

Disadvantages - increased risk of injury, decrease in maximum strength when performed before strength training.

INTERVAL

- More detail on the aerobic page.
- Can work both aerobic & anaerobic systems depending on intensity & W:R ratio.
- Period of high intensity work then period of rest
- Rest allows recovery.

Advantages - quick, easy to manipulate intensity (W:R)

Disadvantages - fatigue quickly.

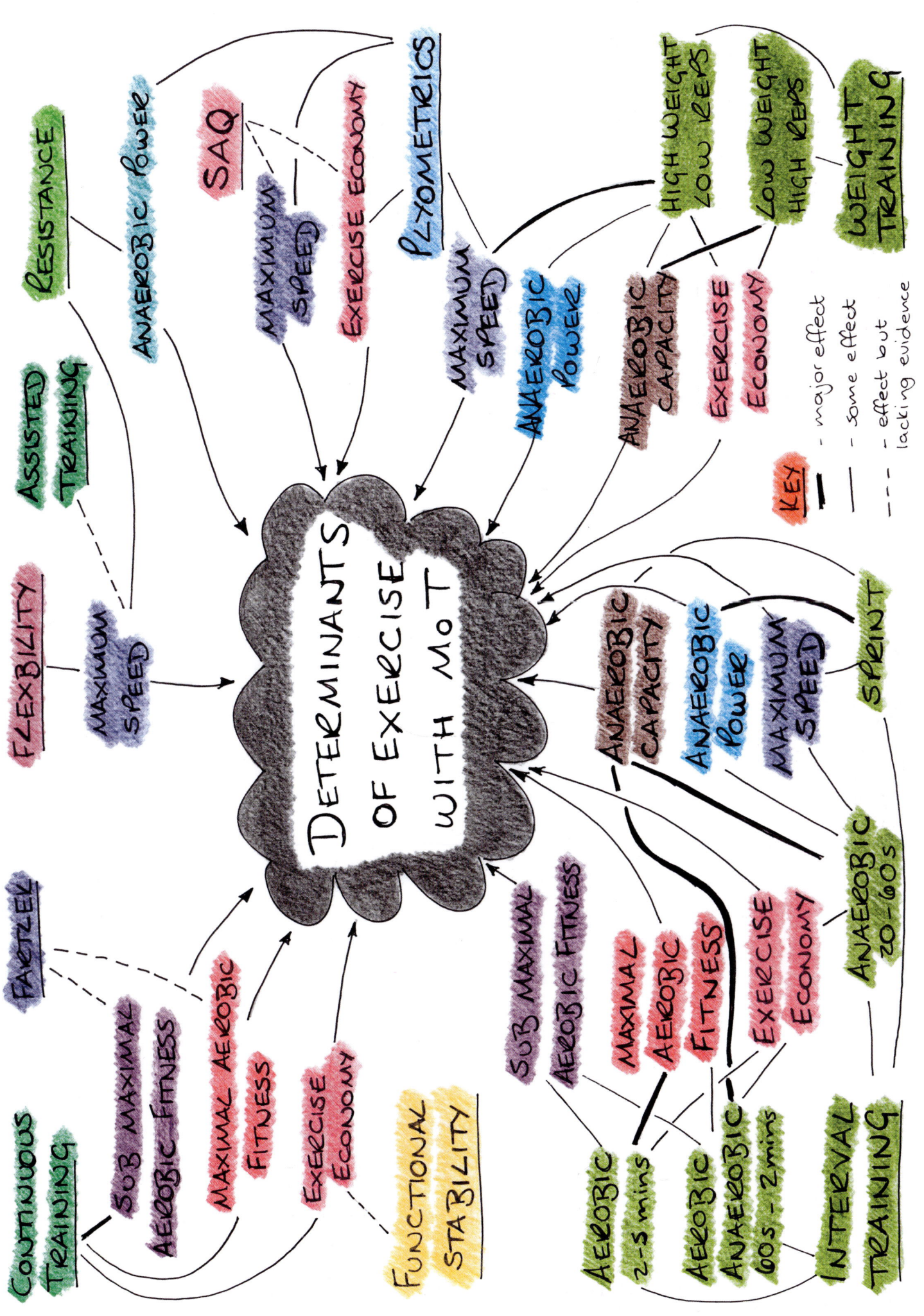

DETERMINANTS OF EXERCISE WITH MoT

RESISTANCE

ANAEROBIC POWER

SAQ

MAXIMUM SPEED

EXERCISE ECONOMY

PLYOMETRICS

MAXIMUM SPEED

ANAEROBIC POWER

ANAEROBIC CAPACITY

EXERCISE ECONOMY

HIGH WEIGHT LOW REPS

LOW WEIGHT HIGH REPS

WEIGHT TRAINING

KEY

— major effect

— some effect

— — — effect but lacking evidence

ASSISTED TRAINING

FLEXIBILITY

MAXIMUM SPEED

ANAEROBIC CAPACITY

ANAEROBIC POWER

MAXIMUM SPEED

SPRINT

ANAEROBIC 20-60s

EXERCISE ECONOMY

FARTLEK

SUB MAXIMAL AEROBIC FITNESS

MAXIMAL AEROBIC FITNESS

EXERCISE ECONOMY

FUNCTIONAL STABILITY

SUB MAXIMAL AEROBIC FITNESS

MAXIMAL AEROBIC FITNESS

EXERCISE ECONOMY

CONTINUOUS TRAINING

AEROBIC 2-5 mins

AEROBIC ANAEROBIC 60s-2mins

INTERVAL TRAINING

PREPARATION FOR PERFORMANCE

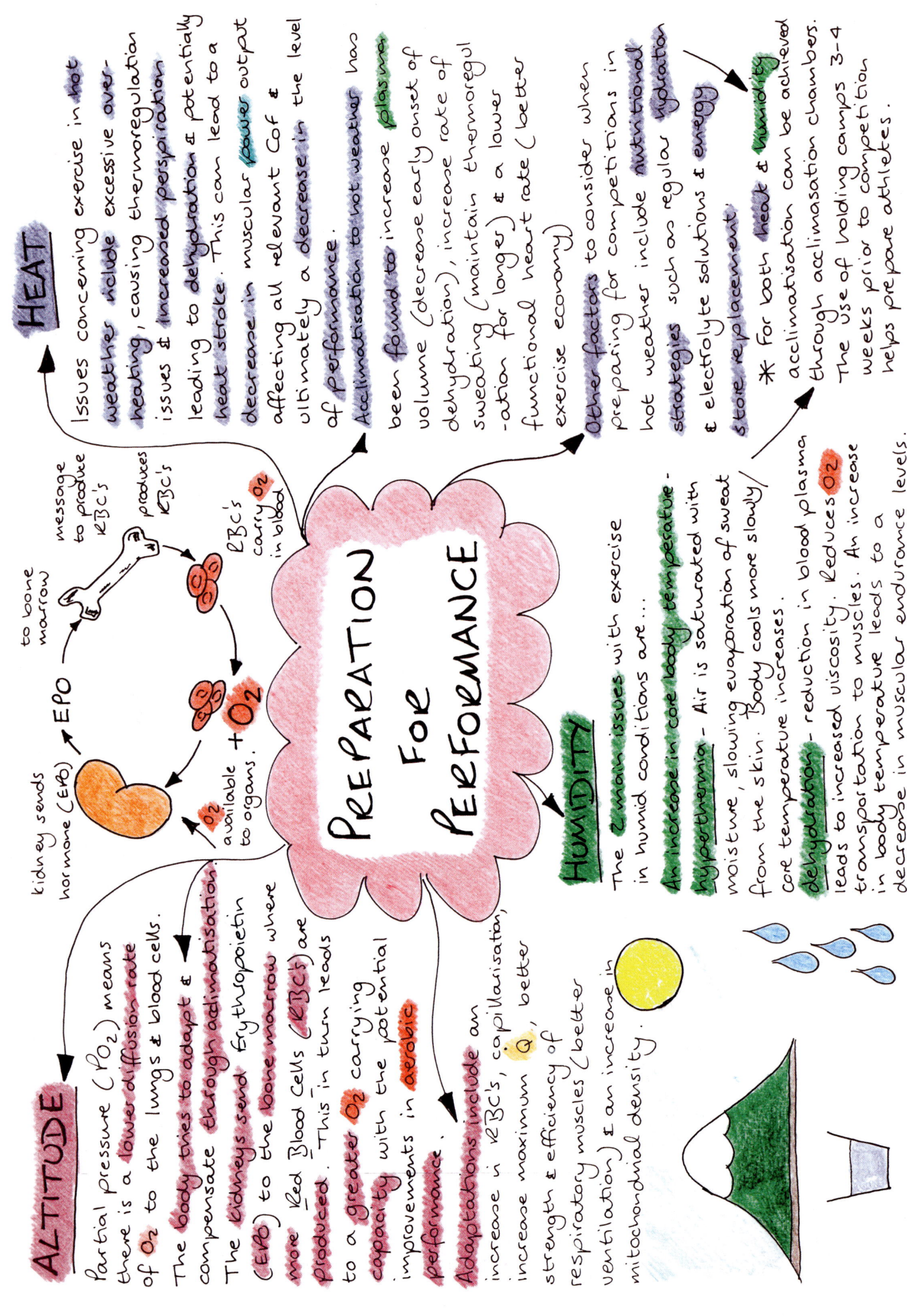

HEAT

Issues concerning exercise in hot weather include excessive over-heating, causing thermoregulation issues & increased perspiration leading to dehydration & potentially heat stroke. This can lead to a decrease in muscular power output affecting all relevant C of & ultimately a decrease in the level of performance.

Acclimatisation to hot weather has been found to increase plasma volume (decrease early onset of dehydration), increase rate of sweating (maintain thermoregulation for longer) & a lower functional heart rate (better exercise economy)

Other factors to consider when preparing for competitions in hot weather include nutritional strategies such as regular hydration & electrolyte solutions & energy store replacement.

* For both heat & humidity acclimatisation can be achieved through acclimatisation chambers. The use of holding camps 3-4 weeks prior to competition helps prepare athletes.

ALTITUDE

Partial pressure (PO₂) means there is a lower diffusion rate of O₂ to the lungs & blood cells.

The body tries to adapt & compensate through acclimatisation. The kidneys send Erythropoietin (EPO) to the bone marrow where more Red Blood Cells (RBC's) are produced. This in turn leads to a greater O₂ carrying capacity with the potential improvements in aerobic performance.

Adaptations include an increase in RBC's, capillarisation, increase maximum Q, better strength & efficiency of respiratory muscles (better ventilation) & an increase in mitochondrial density.

kidney sends hormone (EPO) → EPO → message to produce RBC's → to bone marrow → produces RBC's → RBC's carry O₂ in blood → + O₂ available to organs.

HUMIDITY

The 2 main issues with exercise in humid conditions are...

An increase in core body temperature - hyperthermia - Air is saturated with moisture, slowing evaporation of sweat from the skin. Body cools more slowly/ core temperature increases.

dehydration - reduction in blood plasma leads to increased viscosity. Reduces O₂ transportation to muscles. An increase in body temperature leads to a decrease in muscular endurance levels.

84

STRATEGIES FOR SPEEDING UP RECOVERY

Learn 5...
- Cooling Down
- Compression Clothing
- Massage
- Ice Baths
- Cryotherapy

Contemporary Recovery Methods

* More detail also on pages looking at

MASSAGE

The timing of post-exercise massage is controversial; some suggest it is beneficial within the first 2 hours to reduce DOMS after induced eccentric exercise. eg- downhill running.

Other studies suggest if massage is given too early, it can increase recovery time, especially if there is significant inflammation.

Massage has been found to encourage, increase O_2 & vital nutrient delivery, breakdown of tissue permeability, improve tissue scar tissue & improve tissue elasticity, all potentially reducing recovery time.

ICE BATHS

Have a similar physiological response to active recovery without expending extra energy, caused by hydrostatic pressure effects on the body's fluid in the immersed areas.

Possible benefits include... stimulation of muscle cell activity, speeding up repair of muscle fibres, constriction of blood vessels, reducing swelling & tissue breakdown & assisting in the flushing of waste products (lactate). The use of contrast temperature water therapy has also been shown to substantially reduce blood lactate concentration & heart rate.

CRYOTHERAPY

Usually takes place in walk-in chambers. Liquid nitrogen used to cool air to -110°C & -190°C. Minimises recovery session, usually 2-4 mins. Benefits include... reduction of inflammation, lower levels of cell damage. Some recent research shows muscle pain reduced in 80% of cases.

COOLING DOWN

An active cool down is more effective for promoting post-exercise recovery than a passive cool down, involving no activity.

It helps accelerate dispersion of lactate in blood, recovery of pH to resting levels, recovery of Cardiovascular & Respiratory systems & reduce the effects of DOMS.

It should involve low/moderate aerobic element + static stretches. (benefits not fully conclusive).

COMPRESSION CLOTHING

Compression garments have been reported to help with faster recovery of muscle function, particularly after intense eccentric power or resistance exercise, & so most beneficial post exercise rather than during exercise.

Benefits include a decrease in post-exercise oedema/water retention/ swelling, an increase in the removal of waste products, blood flow & venous return & a decrease in concentrations of creatine kinase.

2.2: Preparation and training methods in relation to maintaining and improving physical activity and performance

1. To maintain appropriate intensity levels, sports performers try to minimise the build-up of lactate.

   a. Describe what is meant by the lactate threshold. (2 marks)

   b. Explain the physiological effects of training and/or performing above the lactate threshold. (4 marks)

   c. Describe a method of training that would benefit a performer by raising the lactate threshold. (3 marks)

2. Discuss the suitability of testing a games players aerobic capacity using the Multi-stage Fitness Test or the Yo-yo intermittent Test. (8 marks)

3. Describe three strategies that could be used to minimise the effects of DOMS. (6 marks)

4. Outline the purpose and procedures for a gas analysis test. (4 marks)

5. Assess whether altitude training is beneficial for developing aerobic endurance. (8 marks)

6. Outline issues with regards to performing in humid conditions. (3 marks)

7. With reference to the listed principles of training that follow overpage:

   a. Define each principle. (3 marks)

   b. Describe how the principles of training can be applied successfully in a training programme. (3 marks)

Specificity:

Progressive Overload:

Reversibility:

8. **Explain** the importance of having an efficient exercise economy as an endurance athlete.   **(4 marks)**

9. **Define** the following components of fitness:

a. Anaerobic capacity   **(1 mark)**

b. VO2max.   **(1 mark)**

c. Submaximal exercise   **(1 mark)**

d. Agility   **(1 mark)**

10. An elite sprinter is using her heart rate (HR) as one way of monitoring intensity in training. Her resting HR is 55 bpm and maximum HR is 180 bpm.

Using the Karvonen formula:

a. **Calculate** the sprinters HR reserve.   **(2 marks)**

b. **Calculate** the sprinters lowest training HR (80% of max. HR).

(2 marks)

c. **Calculate** 90% of max. HR.   **(2 marks)**

11. **Describe** an advantages and disadvantage of plyometric training for a netball player. **(2 marks)**

Total marks for 2.2: Training   /60

2.3: Injury prevention and the rehabilitation of injury

What students need to learn	Yes	Nearly	No
2.3.1: Knowledge and understanding of the different classifications of common sporting injuries.			
2.3.2: Acute injuries: cruciate ligament injury; soft tissue damage, sprain, Achilles tendon injury, fracture, dislocation.			
2.3.3: Overuse injuries: strain, shin splints (periostitis), tendonitis (including tennis elbow and golfers elbow), stress fractures.			
2.3.4: Prevention of injuries: Conditioning, muscle balance, technique, protective equipment, managing risks.			
2.3.5: Rehabilitation from injuries: Contemporary recovery methods and timescales for return to play for injuries in 11.3.1, e.g. ultrasounds, physiotherapy, hyperbaric chambers, oxygen tents, compression garments, ice baths, nutrition, climate chambers, cryotherapy. POLICE — Protection, Optimal Loading, Ice, Compression, Elevation. RICE — Rest, Ice, Compression, Elevation. Advantages and disadvantages of rehabilitation strategies.			

FRACTURE

- Acute fractures (not a stress fracture - that is an overuse injury) occur suddenly as a result of direct impact, fall or a violent twisting movement.

- These fractures are more common in collision (rugby) or contact (football) sports. They can however occur in non contact sports (such as skiing) after a fall.

The 2 main types of fractures are...

OPEN & CLOSED

OPEN

A compound fracture where the broken bone pierces the skin. This increases the risk of infection - Bad.

CLOSED

The bone breaks but does not pierce the skin.

2 types...

SIMPLE - a straight break.

GREENSTICK - the bone bends & breaks on one side. Very common in children.

ACUTE INJURIES

An Acute injury occurs suddenly & can be the result of twisting, turning, falling (explosive movements) or from collisions (eg tackle)

CRUCIATE LIGAMENT INJURY

- The cruciate ligaments are located within the knee & attach the femur to the tibia.

- Both the Anterior Cruciate Ligament (ACL) & Posterior Cruciate Ligament (PCL) are essential in stabilising the knee joint & prevent Anterior-Posterior displacement of the tibia & femur.

- Of the 2, the ACL is more commonly injured & generally occurs when your foot is planted on the ground & a sudden force (a tackle) hits your knee & bends it backwards. It can also occur in twisting or side to side movements.

Increased in numbers with 'blade' studded boots - allowed less lateral foot movement. Very common in football, rugby, netball & skiing.

PCL

ACL

89

SOFT TISSUE DAMAGE

- These injuries include any trauma to the skin (lacerations & abrasions).

- Common injuries include cuts where bleeding becomes an issue, strains (muscular tears), sprains (joint injuries) & contusions (bruising).

- The treatment & recovery process for these injuries varies & depends on the severity of the damage. More on pages 92-94.

- These injuries occur in a wide range of sports, including...

Laceration - a cut inflicted in Boxing from a punch.

Contusion - a broken/damaged blood vessel caused from a big tackle in rugby.

ACUTE INJURIES II

SPRAIN

Is a tear of a ligament, so decreasing stability & support of a joint. 3 common areas where sprains occur include...

Ankle - inversion/eversion (twisting

Knee - sudden twist damages collateral ligaments

Wrist - falling on outstretched hand

DISLOCATION

- Occurs due to trauma dislodging the bone from a joint.

- This type of injury is more likely to occur & performers are more susceptible when the muscles & tendons that surround a joint are weak, or if there is an imbalance.

- Common sites for dislocation include fingers, shoulder & knee

- Frequently occurs in rugby & cricket from the impact of the ball, or rugby from a tackle or collapsed scrum.

ACHILLES TENDON

Is the largest tendon in the body & joins calcaneus (heel bone & gastrocnemius)

Common in sports where have to accelerate quickly, decelerate quickly and/or pivot, as with sprinters. Generally occur when performer pushes off & lifts foot, accompanied with pain.

OVERUSE INJURIES

STRESS FRACTURES

Are a micro-fracture caused by too much stress on a bone & trauma that gradually develops over time.

Additional risk factors include...

- Repetitive high impact exercise
- High training frequency & intensity
- Not adhering to appropriate application of the principles of training.
  - Poor nutrition
  - Improper technique
  - Improper clothing/technique.

Most common stress fractures include...
- Metatarsal bones in the foot (long distance runner)
- Vertebrae (fast bowler - cricket).

TENDONITIS

Repetitive loading of a tendon, exceeding ability to handle load. Caused by...

- High training frequency & intensity
- Biomechanical errors in technique
- Training surfaces
- Inappropriate equipment
- Muscle imbalance
- Inadequate recovery time.

Common tendonitis injuries occur in the knee, achilles & elbow.

GOLFERS ELBOW (inside)

Or medial epicondylitis causes pain & inflammation on medial part of elbow (inside). Not just in golf, racquet sports also where clench fist & repeatedly use wrists.

TENNIS ELBOW (outside)

Or lateral epicondylitis causes pain & inflammation of the tendon that attaches on the lateral part of the elbow. Not just common in tennis, swinging racquet/bat sports eg - cricket.

OVERUSE

injuries are more subtle & occur over time, making them more difficult to diagnose & treat. Generally caused by repetitive micro-trauma to soft tissue, joints & bones as a result of poor technique, over training surfaces, equipment or returning too soon after injury.

STRAIN

'A tear' or pulling of a muscle or tendon. It is often an acute injury, although without proper preparation & rehabilitation, chronic pain & recurrence can occur.

Strains tend to occur in muscles that cross 2 joints, such as the quadricep/p hamstring/gp, groin & gastrocnemius.

Regardless of severity, proper rehabilitation is required to ensure full recovery & limit the chance of recurrence.

SHIN SPLINTS

Aka Periostitis. A condition where there is inflammation of the periosteum that covers the bone (tibia).

Repeated stress in the form of running, jumping & turning on firm surfaces can lead to shin splints. Can also be caused by weight training.

Symptoms include - swelling, intense pain & can be tender to touch.

Performers who train & play on hard surfaces excessively are at risk of chronic periostitis eg - runners.

PREVENTION OF INJURIES

MUSCLE BALANCE

- Muscle imbalance results from weakness, poor flexibility and/or low/poor endurance.
- Common injuries caused by muscle imbalances include...
- Hamstring muscle tightness/weakness can put strain on the ACL, quadriceps & cause knee pain.
- Rotator cuff injuries can also be caused by over-tight pectoral muscles.
- A balanced strength programme is required to minimise injury.

PROTECTIVE EQUIPMENT

- Protective equipment in elite sport is generally enforced by most teams, clubs, NGB's & sponsors, to ensure unnecessary injuries are minimised.
- eg helmets for batting in cricket, helmets for cycling, mouthguards in hockey, rugby & boxing, correct gloves in boxing.

MANAGING RISKS

- NGB's conduct a review of rules in order to prevent injury. eg law adjustment to scrums in rugby

TECHNIQUE

- Practising/training with repetitive poor technique can lead to injuries such as stress fractures & tendonitis.
- Using biomechanical analysis apps & a qualified coach can help to alleviate any issues with technique to minimise injuries & maximise performance.

CONDITIONING

- Applying a structured periodised yearly plan & the application of appropriate principles of training (progressive overload) will ensure a performers body is ready for the demands of their sport.
- More injuries occur in the latter stages of a game, therefore conditioning is crucial.
- A study published in 'British Journal of Sports Medicine in 2018 stated there was a significant reduction of acute injuries as a result of strength training. This could be a result of increased strength & size of muscles & adjacent tissue, a decrease in critical joint loads & improved coordination, as well as having psychological benefits. eg increased confidence.

REHABILITATION FROM INJURIES

P – protection. Unload & shield the injury for short periods.

O/L – optimal loading. Replaces 'rest' with a more balanced and incremental rehabilitation programme.

I – ice. Reduces inflammation.

C – compression. Support the injured area.

E – elevation. Above the level of the heart to reduce blood flow to the injured area & increase the rate of venous return.

* learn this and what each letter means.

A study in 2014 in the British Journal of Sports Medicine highlighted the application of **POLICE**.

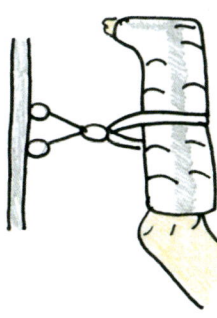

- For most soft tissue injuries **RICE** has always been the widespread acronym applied for rehabilitation.

R – rest
I – ice
C – compression
E – elevation

However, the term **REST** has caused issue with some Sports Scientists as some recent studies suggest that some type of mobilisation / mobility exercises will increase the rate of recovery, as well as decreasing muscular atrophy & scar tissue. The level of oxygen delivery to the injured site also increased.

- increased blood flow.

CLASSES OF SOFT TISSUE INJURIES

1st degree – minor tear. Recovery approx 1 week.

2nd degree – partial tear. Recovery between 2-6 weeks.

3rd degree – complete tear. Recovery between 6-8 weeks.

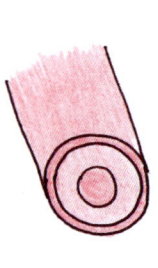
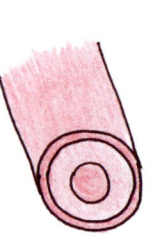

HYPERBARIC CHAMBERS

Hyperbaric therapy is a treatment where 100% O_2 is administered under pressure greater than the atmospheric O_2 pressure.

The process pressurises the blood vessels within the body for 60-120 mins, to accelerate the recovery of soft tissue micro-tears, hence decreasing the risk/effect of DOMS.

The idea is to recover more quickly, exercise for longer to help maximise performance levels.

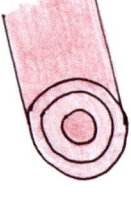

CONTEMPORARY RECOVERY METHODS

ICE BATHS

Believed to decrease/reduce inflammation & increase recovery rates. Blood vessels constrict & then dilate when you get out. This process helps to flush out metabolic waste at the end of an intense training session or performance.

ULTRASOUNDS

The use of ultrasonic waves causes vibration of the tissue, especially those that contain collagen. This increases muscle temperature, reduces pain, muscle spasms & promotes the healing process.

As it promotes blood flow, it is recommended that this procedure is conducted until after the initial 48 hr inflammation period.

MASSAGE (PHYSIO)

This is widely used as a recovery strategy to reduce muscle soreness & to stimulate blood flow. However, most evidence does not support massage as an effective method to improve/increase recovery of functional performance.

It is thought that massage is more beneficial for prevention & management of injury, as well as providing a psychological boost to the performer.

COMPRESSION GARMENTS

Increases blood flow to muscles & increases venous return to disperse waste products.

Better used post exercise for recovery rather than during. Thought to reduce intramuscular space available for swelling, thereby decreasing DOMS.

CONTEMPORARY RECOVERY METHODS II

There are many different recovery methods discussed here & on the previous page. All have the same aim of decreasing recovery time to aid performance.

HYDROTHERAPY

Cold water therapy has been proven to reduce muscle soreness & increase/improve recovery times.

In addition, contrast water therapy for a duration of 14-15 mins has been shown to improve performance.

Research has shown that contrast therapy should be (1:1 & 7 rotations of hot/cold immersions

CRYOTHERAPY

Each session can last between 2-4 mins & involves exposing the body to extremely low temperatures generated by liquid nitrogen. The theory behind this method, explains that vasoconstriction of blood vessels occurs, reducing blood flow. Once treatment finishes, vessels then dilate, flushing waste products from the body, assisting the lymphatic system & improving recovery.

OXYGEN TENT

Similar to hyperbaric chambers, however O2 tents refer more to supplemental O2 at ambient pressure. Both methods increase arterial oxygenation to increase/improve recovery rates.

HYPOXIC TENTS

A hypoxic tent tries to simulate high altitude conditions. Using this method, performers do not have to travel to areas of high altitude.

This method aims to increase EPO production & increase mitochondrial efficiency.

Hypoxic tents historically have been used for preparation for events. However, more recently Exercise Physiologists have opted for a 'live high, train low' method (LHTL). Using the method this way, athletes train at the specific altitude, but recover at a faster rate in hypoxic conditions.

2.3: Injury prevention and the rehabilitation of injury

1. **Describe**, using examples, the difference between an acute injury and an overuse injury. **(4 marks)**

2. **Identify** (a) and **classify** (b) the descriptions of injuries below:

   i)   Swelling and inflammation of a tendon   **(2 marks)**
   ii)   Fatigue-induced small crack in a weight-bearing bone.   **(2 marks)**
   iii)   A force that pulls or stretches a muscle or tendon.   **(2 marks)**
   iv)   Separation of articulating bones.   **(2 marks)**
   v)   Inflammation of the periosteum.   **(2 marks)**
   vi)   Stretching or tearing of ligaments that causes swelling.   **(2 marks)**

3. **Describe** four ways in which sports performers can try and prevent injuries. **(8 marks)**

4. **Outline** the benefits of elevating a soft-tissue injury above the level of the heart. **(2 marks)**

5. **Discuss** the use of hyperbaric chambers v hypoxic tents in the recovery from injuries. **(8 marks)**

6. **Evaluate** the advantages and disadvantages of using POLICE as a recovery strategy. **(8 marks)**

Total marks for 2.3: Injury prevention and the rehabilitation of injury: /42

Biomechanics

2.4: Linear Motion What you need to learn.	Yes	Nearly	No
2.4.1: Knowledge and understanding of the factors associated with linear motion and the application of definitions, equations, calculations and units of measurement in a sporting context.			
2.4.2: Calculation of the distance and displacement, speed and average speed, velocity and acceleration. Speed = distance/time ($s = d/t$) Velocity = displacement/time or distance/time (m/s) Acceleration = (final velocity — initial velocity)/time taken (m/s)			
2.4.3: Plot, label and interpret graphs of motion. To include distance/time, speed/time graphs and velocity/time graphs.			

2.5: Angular Motion What you need to learn.	Yes	Nearly	No
2.5.1: Knowledge and understanding of how angular motion is applied in a sporting context.			
2.5.2: Factors affecting moment of inertia: mass and distribution of mass from axis of rotation.			
2.5.3: Effects of increasing or decreasing the moment of inertia when rotating about an axes (whole body or specific joint).			
2.5.4: Conservation of angular momentum during flight, moment of inertia and its relationship with angular velocity.			

2.6: Projectile Motion What students need to learn	Yes	Nearly	No
2.6.1: Knowledge, understanding and application of projectile motion in refining technique in different sporting contexts.			
2.6.2: Forces acting during flight that affect projectile motion: gravity, air resistance and lift forces.			
2.6.3: Factors that determine the horizontal displacement of a projectile: velocity of release, height of release, angle of release.			
2.6.4: Technique modification through the application of technology by the performer and coach in order to improve performance.			

2.7: Fluid Mechanics What you need to learn.	Yes	Nearly	No
2.7.1: Knowledge, understanding and application of aerodynamics and hydrodynamics to appropriate sports contexts.			
2.7.2: Factors affecting fluid friction and air resistance: velocity, drag force, mass, streamlining and surface characteristics of body.			
2.7.3: Interaction of lift forces with objects: upward and downward lift forces, angle of attack and the Bernoulli effect.			
2.7.4: Types of spin: topspin, backspin, sidespin. Magnus effect and how they impact on flight path and bounce.			
2.7.5: Principles of fluid mechanics and how it has influenced technological advancements in technique modification, clothing/suits, equipment/apparatus.			

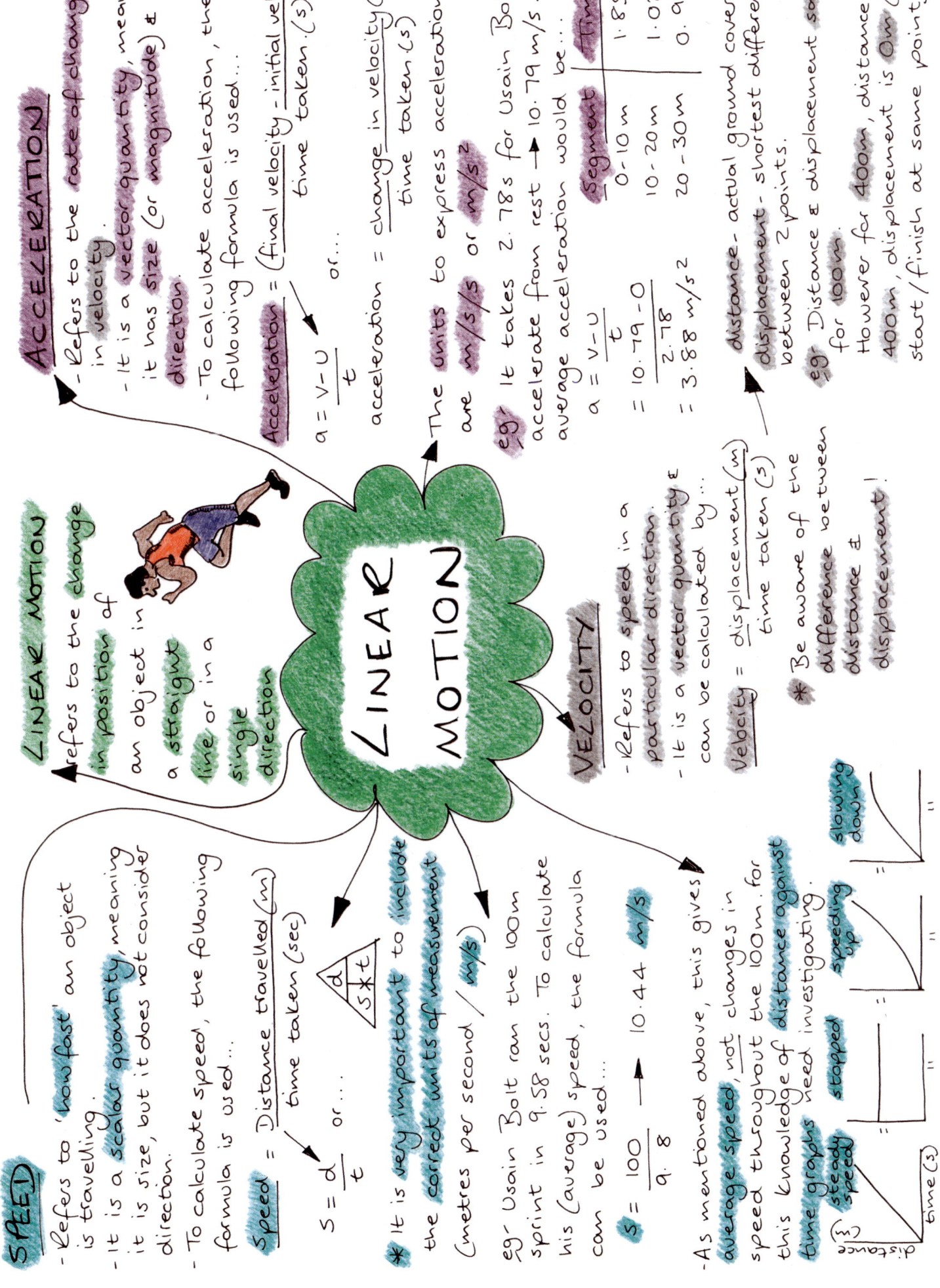

ACCELERATION
- Refers to the rate of change in velocity
- It is a vector quantity, meaning it has size (or magnitude) & direction
- To calculate acceleration, the following formula is used... (m/s)

$$\text{Acceleration} = \frac{(\text{final velocity} - \text{initial velocity})}{\text{time taken (s)}}$$

$$a = \frac{V - U}{t} \quad \text{or...}$$

$$\text{acceleration} = \frac{\text{change in velocity (m/s)}}{\text{time taken (s)}}$$

The units to express acceleration are m/s/s or m/s²

eg. It takes 2.78s for Usain Bolt to accelerate from rest → 10.79 m/s. The average acceleration would be...

$$a = \frac{V - U}{t}$$
$$= \frac{10.79 - 0}{2.78}$$
$$= 3.88 \ m/s^2$$

Segment	Time
0-10m	1.85 s
10-20m	1.02 s
20-30m	0.91 s

distance - actual ground covered
displacement - shortest difference between 2 points.

eg. Distance & displacement same for 100m.
However for 400m, distance is 400m, displacement is 0m (as start/finish at same point).

LINEAR MOTION
- refers to the change in position of an object in a straight line or in a single direction

LINEAR MOTION

VELOCITY
- Refers to speed in a particular direction
- It is a vector quantity & can be calculated by...

$$\text{Velocity} = \frac{\text{displacement (m)}}{\text{time taken (s)}}$$

* Be aware of the difference between distance & displacement!

SPEED
- Refers to 'how fast' an object is travelling.
- It is a scalar quantity, meaning it is size, but it does not consider direction.
- To calculate speed, the following formula is used...

$$\text{Speed} = \frac{\text{Distance travelled (m)}}{\text{time taken (sec)}}$$

$$s = \frac{d}{t} \quad \text{or...}$$

$$\frac{d}{s \times t}$$

* It is very important to include the correct units of measurement (metres per second / m/s)

eg. Usain Bolt ran the 100m sprint in 9.58 secs. To calculate his (average) speed, the formula can be used...

$$s = \frac{100}{9.58} \rightarrow 10.44 \ m/s$$

- As mentioned above, average speed, not changes in speed throughout the 100m for this knowledge of distance against need investigating.

the graphs

steady speed   stopped   speeding up   slowing down

distance (m) / time (s)

ANGULAR MOTION

MOMENT OF INERTIA

- Inertia is the 'amount of force required to move a mass in a straight line.'

- Moment of inertia (or rotational inertia) uses the same concept, but relates to rotational movement.

- Therefore, the further away a mass is from the axis of rotation, the more 'spread out' the mass is. This would increase the moment of inertia & more force would be needed to move it/slow down.

eg a gymnast performing a somersault in an open position (arms & legs extended) will have a large moment of inertia as the mass of the body will spread away from the axis of rotation, & therefore will spin slowly.

ANGULAR MOTION

- Angular motion is defined as... the motion of a body/mass about a fixed point or axis. (rotating or spinning action). The same principles in terms of velocity, displacement & acceleration used for LINEAR MOTION apply to angular motion.

As the gymnast looks to land, the limbs will move out & away from the axis of rotation, increasing MI & decreasing angular velocity in order to slow the spin/rotations so they can land safely.

ANGULAR MOMENTUM

- Refers to the product of angular velocity & moment of inertia.

- ANGULAR MOMENTUM = MI × ANGULAR VELOCITY

Therefore if MI increases, angular velocity decreases & vice versa, providing there is no other force acting on the object. eg air resistance. If there are no outside forces acting on the rotating object/body, then angular momentum is conserved (as there is no change in total angular momentum).

eg a gymnast performing a somersault will tuck their body in to decrease MI & increase angular velocity. ie increase rate of spin/rotations.

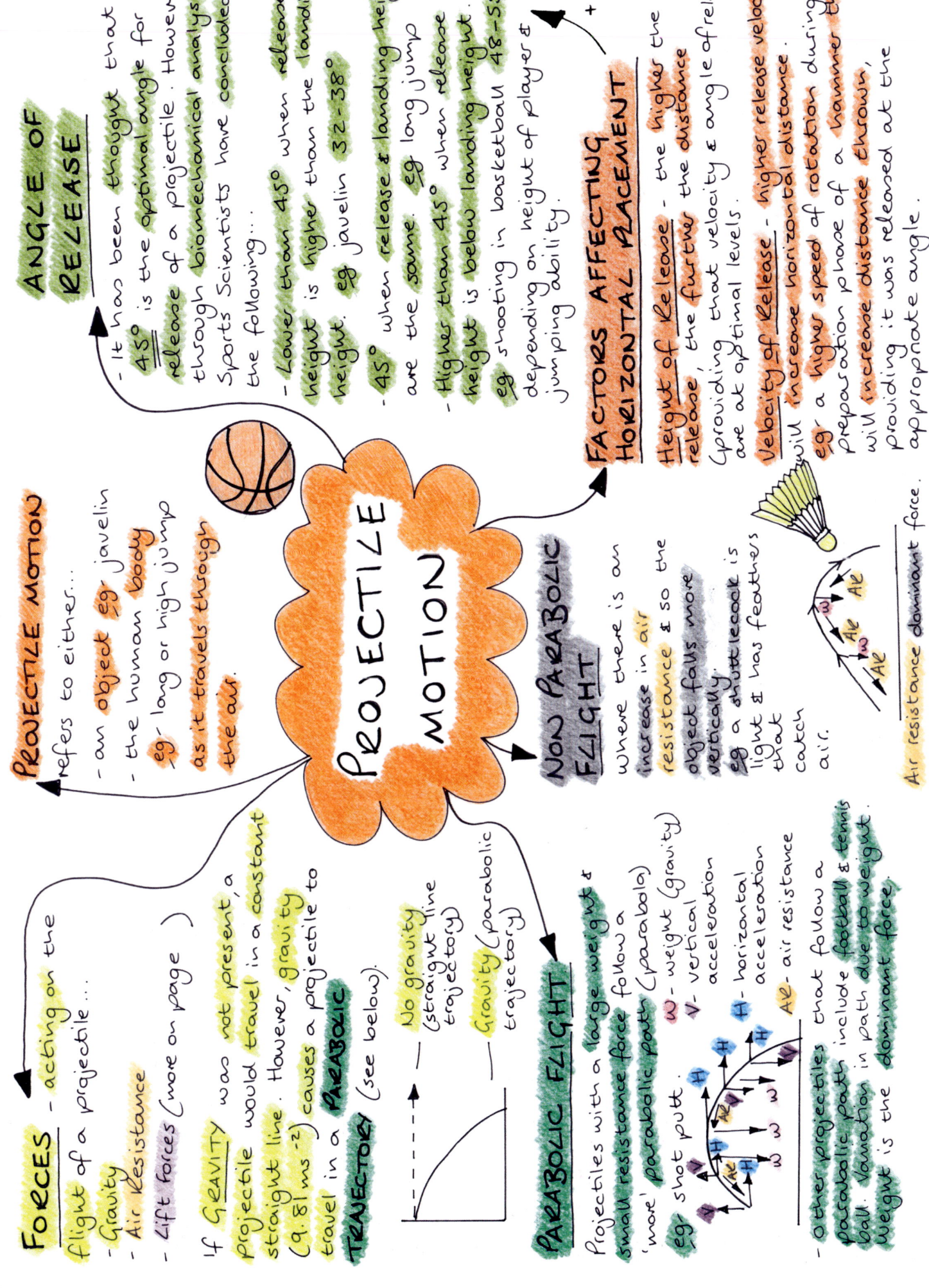

PROJECTILE MOTION

ANGLE OF RELEASE

- It has been thought that 45° is the optimal angle for release of a projectile. However, through biomechanical analysis Sports Scientists have concluded the following...

- Lower than 45° when release height is higher than the landing height. eg javelin 32-38°

- Higher than 45° when release height is below landing height 48-55°

- 45° when release & landing height are the same. eg long jump

eg shooting in basketball depending on height of player & jumping ability.

FACTORS AFFECTING HORIZONTAL PLACEMENT

Height of Release - the higher the release, the further the distance (providing that velocity & angle of release are at optimal levels.

Velocity of Release - higher release velocity will increase horizontal distance. eg a higher speed of rotation during the preparation phase of a hammer throw will increase distance thrown, providing it was released at the appropriate angle.

PROJECTILE MOTION

refers to either...
- an object eg javelin
- the human body
eg - long or high jump
as it travels through the air.

FORCES - acting on the flight of a projectile...

- Gravity
- Air Resistance
- Lift forces (more on page)

If GRAVITY was not present, a projectile would travel in a constant straight line. However, gravity (9.81 ms^{-2}) causes a projectile to travel in a PARABOLIC (see below).

TRAJECTORY

— No gravity (straight line trajectory)

— Gravity (parabolic trajectory)

NON PARABOLIC FLIGHT

where there is an increase in air resistance & so the object falls more vertically. eg a shuttlecock is light & has feathers that catch air.

Air resistance dominant force.

PARABOLIC FLIGHT

Projectiles with a large weight & small resistance force follow a 'more' parabolic path (parabola)

W - weight (gravity)
V - vertical acceleration
H - horizontal acceleration
AR - air resistance

eg shot putt

- other projectiles that follow a parabolic path include football & tennis ball. Variation in path due to weight. Weight is the dominant force.

HYDRODYNAMICS

- Refers to the flow of water around a projectile which can influence the speed & direction of travel.
- Ways in which swimmers can reduce drag — streamline body position & flat in water.
  - lean bodies
  - minimise turbulent flow by...
- wear tight fitting swimsuits
- swimming hats
- remove hair
- maximise 15m distance underwater at the start & on turns to reduce drag from turbulence on the surface. (Dolphin Kick).

The Speedo LZR Racer Swimsuit is now banned! Why?
- technical doping
- compressed the swimmers body into a streamlined tube.
- trapped air 'inside suit', adding buoyancy to the swimmer & ultimately reducing the level/amount of drag.

Fluid mechanics considers objects that move through the AIR (Aerodynamics) or WATER (Hydrodynamics). It involves the forces acting against moving objects within these mediums & how they slow them down.

FLUID MECHANICS

AERODYNAMICS

- Refers to the flow of air around a projectile which can influence the speed & direction of travel. (Aerodynamic drag or drag force).
- Air resistance can be affected by several factors, including...
- Velocity — an increase in velocity leads to increased air resistance opposing the object.
- Shape — the more aerodynamic the object, the lower the resistance.
- Cross-Sectional area (Frontal) — the smaller the frontal cross-sectional area, the lower the air resistance. eg. crouching down low when cycling downhill.
- Smoothness of surface — the smoother the surface, the lower the air resistance. (See below)

Direction of travel

The wake is an low pressure zone. It is larger for a rough surface ball, therefore more drag.

This is the same concept with cycling helmets. The more stream-lined (decreased frontal cross sectional area) — leads to a decreased low pressure zone to reduce drag & increase speed.

Goes further

Direction of travel → turbulence

'less wake & so less drag-low pressure zone minimised.'

However, with a golf ball, the dimples have been designed to create an attach-detach-attach again system that creates tiny pockets of turbulence so that the air flow is close to the ball, decreasing the wake & decreasing the low pressure zone.

wake

smooth

rough

Air flow

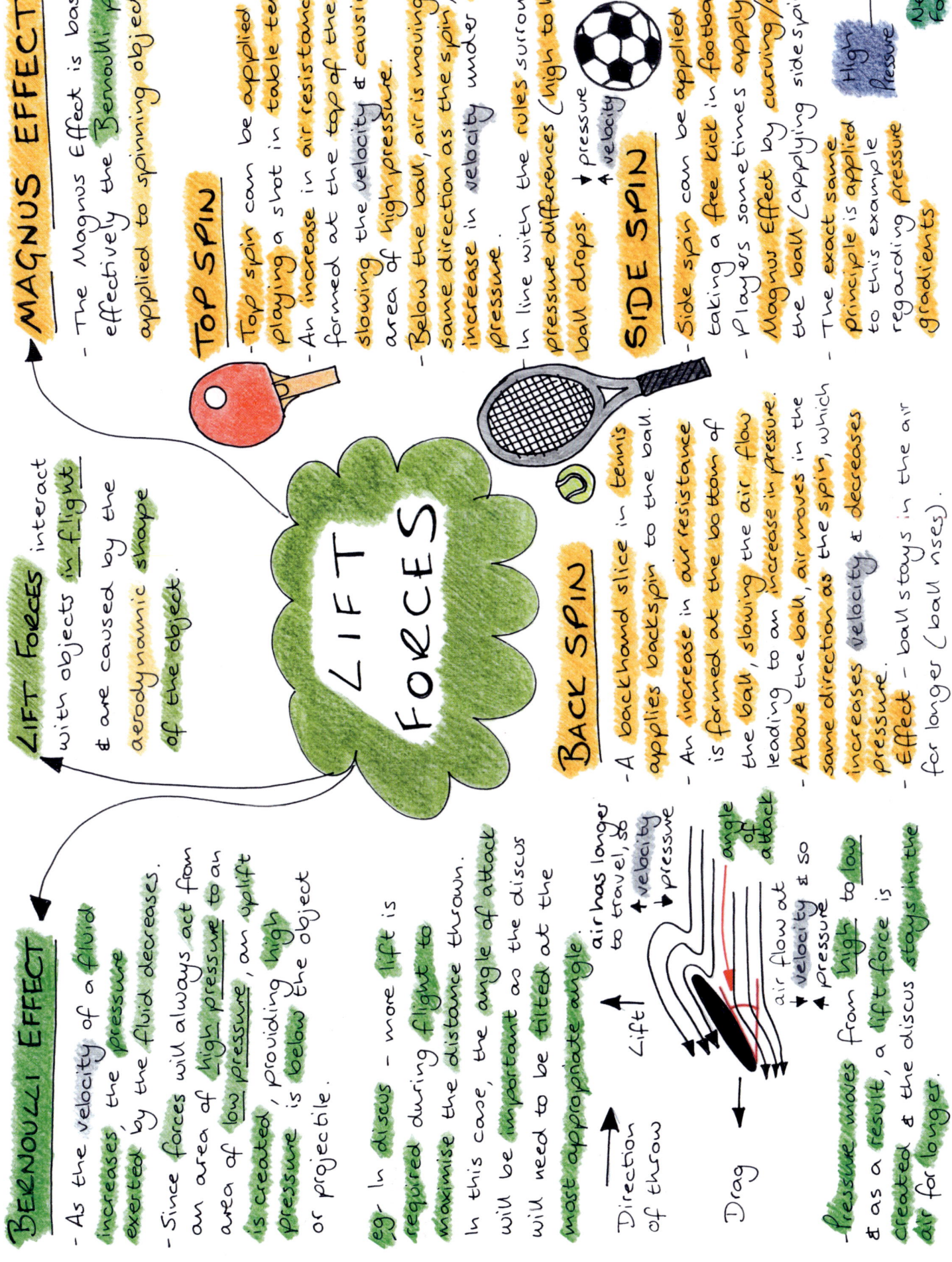

MAGNUS EFFECT

- The Magnus Effect is basically/ effectively the Bernoulli principle applied to spinning objects.

TOP SPIN

- Top spin can be applied when playing a shot in table tennis.
- An increase in air resistance is formed at the top of the ball, slowing the velocity & causing an area of high pressure.
- Below the ball, air is moving in the same direction as the spin, with an increase in velocity under lower pressure.
- In line with the rules surrounding pressure differences (high to low), the ball drops.

↑ pressure
↓ velocity
↓ velocity of strike

↑ pressure
↑ velocity

SIDE SPIN

- Side spin can be applied when taking a free kick in football.
- Players sometimes apply the Magnus Effect by curving/curling the ball (applying side spin).
- The exact same principle is applied to this example regarding pressure gradients.

Low Pressure

Net Force

High Pressure

LIFT FORCES

LIFT FORCES interact with objects in flight & are caused by the aerodynamic shape of the object.

BACK SPIN

- A backhand slice in tennis applies backspin to the ball.
- An increase in air resistance is formed at the bottom of the ball, slowing the air flow leading to an increase in pressure.
- Above the ball, air moves in the same direction as the spin, which increases velocity & decreases pressure.
- Effect - ball stays in the air for longer (ball rises).

BERNOULLI EFFECT

- As the velocity of a fluid increases, the pressure exerted by the fluid decreases.

- Since forces will always act from an area of high pressure to an area of low pressure, an uplift is created, providing high pressure is below the object or projectile.

eg: In discus - more lift is required during flight to maximise the distance thrown. In this case, the angle of attack will be important as the discus will need to be tilted at the most appropriate angle.

air has longer to travel, so ↑ velocity ↓ pressure

angle of attack

air flow at ↑ velocity ↓ pressure

Lift

Direction of throw

Drag

- Pressure moves from high to low & as a result, a lift force is created & the discus stays in the air for longer.

2.4-2.7: Biomechanics

1. The table below shows the breakdown of Usain Bolts 100m sprint performance in the 2008 Beijing Olympics. The table outlines the split times and cumulative times for every 10m.

Splits (10m)	10m plit times (s)	Cumulative time (s)	Average speed (m/s)
0-10	1.85	1.85	
10-20	1.02	2.87	
20-30	0.91	3.78	
30-40	0.87	4.65	
40-50	0.85	5.50	
50-0	0.82	6.32	
60-70	0.82	7.14	
70-80	0.83	7.96	
80-90	0.83	8.79	
90-100	0.90	9.69	
Total Time	9.69	9.69	

a. **Calculate** the average speed for every 10m and the overall average speed for the 100m (write your answer in the table above) **(10 marks)**

Show your working:

b. **Calculate** Usain Bolts acceleration between:

i) 0-20m   **(2 marks)**

ii) 20-50m   **(2 marks)**

iii) 50-70m   **(2 marks)**

iv) 70-100m   **(2 marks)**

v) **Give** reasons for differences in acceleration rates between the two parameters mentioned in i) and ii).   **(3 marks)**

c. Using the grid below, complete the following:

i) **Plot** the results from the table in the distance against time graph below.

                                       (1 mark)

ii) **Shade** the area of the graph where the sprinter accelerated the most.

                                       (1 mark)

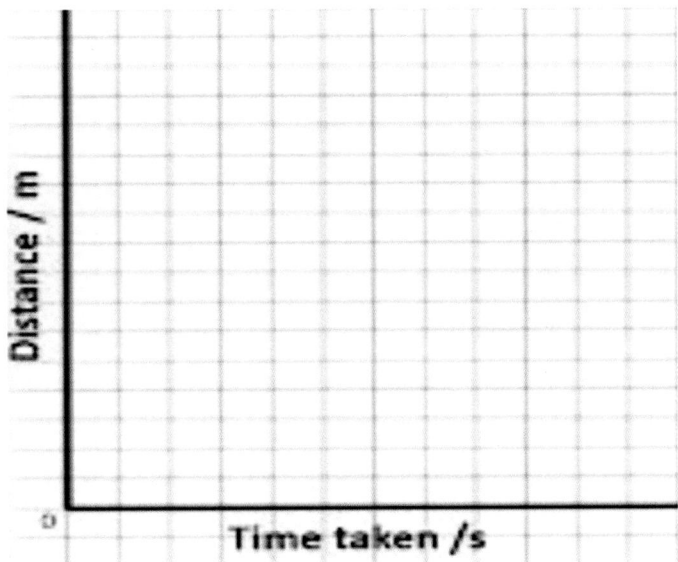

2. The following graphs show displacement against time. Each graph is labelled A to E:

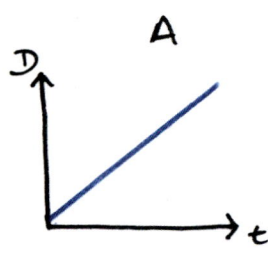

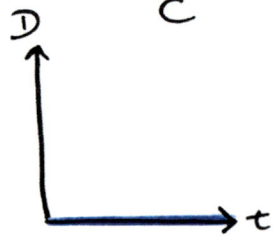

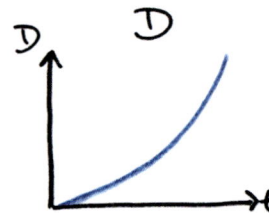

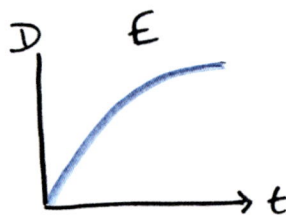

Which graph is displaying the following?

i) Acceleration   (1 mark)

ii) 0 velocity and 0 displacement   (1 mark)

iii) Constant speed   (1 mark)

iv) 0 velocity   (1 mark)

v) Deceleration   (1 mark)

3. The figure below shows an ice skater:

a. **Identify** what makes up a performers moment of inertia? *(2 marks)*

b. Using the figure above, **explain** how the ice skater can adjust their rate of spin. *(4 marks)*

4. **Identify** the factors that affect horizontal displacement. *(3 marks)*

5. The flight paths of different objects can be parabolic or non-parabolic.

a. **Define** parabolic. *(1 mark)*

b. **Describe** the main factors that limit the distance that a golf ball will travel in flight. *(3 marks)*

c. **Compare** the flight of a golf ball with a shuttle cock. *(4 marks)*

6. **Explain** how the angle of release is different with various projectile based sporting activities. *(6 marks)*

7. **Identify** three factors that affect fluid friction and air resistance. *(3 marks)*

8. **State** strategies a swimmer could do to lessen the effect of fluid friction whilst swimming. *(3 marks)*

9. The discus is also an athletic event where maximising horizontal displacement is key to winning the event.

Analyse how the **Bernoulli effect** will affect the flight path and the displacement of the discus. *(8 marks)*

10. In table tennis it is possible to apply spin on the ball when playing various shots.

Examine how the player, using his/her knowledge of the **Magnus effect** apply this?

(8 marks)

Total marks for 2.4-2.7: Biomechanics: /73